.

Praise for
Women Make Great Leaders

The most powerful way to bring positive change is to bring diversity, in all of its forms, together with a common vision and passionate execution. Attracting, developing and promoting great women leaders can be a catalyst for that positive change, and the examples shared in Jill Griffin's work can instruct and inspire us all.

—Mike Sicard,
Chairman & CEO USI

A true 'Master Connector', Jill Griffin has combined together her wisdom, her experience and her passion to share with others her playbook on what's required for EVERYONE to be an amazing leader!

—Lou Diamond
Best-selling author, Master the Art of Connecting

Put the book in the hands of every person you know! It's no secret that women make great leaders, it's a fact. Time everyone learned this first hand.

—Jeffrey W. Hayzlett
Primetime TV & Radio Host, Speaker,
Author and Part-Time Cowboy

When more women sit at the decision making tables, better decisions are made. This book is a valuable resource for any women who wants to step up to the leadership plate and make a bigger mark in her workplace and the world.

—Margie Warrell
Bestselling Author of Stop Playing Safe *and*
Ambassador for Women in Global Business

More Praise for
Women Make Great Leaders

This book is an invaluable guide that will help you—or a woman you care about—tap into your own true leadership potential. Jill Griffin pushes past the myths and misconceptions, and provides smart insights about how professional advancement and achievement really works.

—Dorie Clark
author of Reinventing You *and* Stand Out.
Adjunct professor, Duke University Fuqua School of Business

Not every woman who climbs the corporate ladder will vanish. This amazing book highlights the women who stand in their leadership abilities, no matter the life/career winds that blow. Thank you Jill for highlighting the true impact of women in leadership roles outside the home and community. Here's to all of us continuously pressing forward while we encourage others along the journey and challenge our peers to do the same. Fortitude!

—Ada-Renee Johnson
Head of SWE & Diversity Pipeline, Google, Inc.

Women Make Great Leaders features successful women to motivate all—both men and women. It provides food for thought and tangible action specifics illustrated in achieving women's stories. A must read for people of all ages, genders and life stages.

—Linda L. Golden, JD, PhD
Professor of Marketing and Business, Debt Government and Society
IC2, Humanities Institute and DSEF Fellow
McCombs School of Business
University of Texas-Austin

I've had the good fortune to have been surrounded by very successful women who inspired in me the values of hard work, a big picture attitude and the need to contribute to the success of others. In this book, Jill Griffin uniquely captures what all of us should know about passion, vision, courage and leadership.

—*Arthur R. Emerson*
CEO KLRU, San Antonio, TX

Jill has blazed a leadership trail to the very pinnacle of the corporate world. She obviously took excellent notes along the way. Rather than rest on her laurels, Jill has crafted a thoughtful road map for aspiring women—generously marked with critical signposts. Her tried and true advice is a must read for those who seek to challenge their limits.

—*Honorable Harriet O'Neill*
Justice (Ret.), Supreme Court of Texas

Jill Griffin has written a book for anyone who aspires to become a leader at any level in any organization or any point in their career. She has created a wonderful integration of real-life stories of people. Jill's book transcends categories of people who became successful leaders by learning how to grow and adapt to ever more complex and ambiguous demands of their capabilities with supporting analyses and guidelines to back each story. Supporting several different learning styles, her book is a highly consumable "how-to" grow yourself. It's accessible to all.

—*Bruce Ballengee*
Founder & CEO Pariveda Solutions

More Praise for
Women Make Great Leaders

Jill Griffin's stories of successful leaders will inspire readers to use all of their gifts and talents and rise to every occasion. This book will open doors!

—*Frances Hesselbein,*
President and CEO, Frances Hesselbein Leadership Institute

Jill Griffin has written a masterful primer, one which guides the reader to meld the "secret powers" of females—empathy, patience, respect, and caring to name a few—with a common sense approach to leadership. The organization and concise take-aways are sure to make *Women Make Great Leaders* a trusted go-to resource for emerging leaders of any gender.

—*Susan Kiehl*
Vice President Integrated Fighter Group Product Development,
Lockheed Martin Aeronautics, retired.

WOMEN
MAKE GREAT
LEADERS

WOMEN

MAKE GREAT

LEADERS

Real-World Lessons to Accelerate Your Climb

JILL GRIFFIN

Published by Jill Griffin Books
3818-A Ridgelea Drive, Austin, TX 78731

Copyright © 2017 by JJ Griffin Enterprises, Inc.
Inquiries: jillgriffin.net

Cover design by Justin Esquivel
Book design by Alex Head/Draft Lab LLC
Book logo design by Justin Esquivel
Trademark design by Justin Esquivel

ISBN: 978-0-9969218-2-4

Set in Adobe Garamond Pro

Printed in the United States of America.

"Love is work made visible."
—Kahill Gibran
The Prophet

This book is dedicated to those women and men who throughout the annals of time have believed that women make great leaders, and have acted accordingly.

CONTENTS

WELCOME TO BECOMING!

Y ou are on the road to becoming an exceptional leader, and it's a privilege to accompany you on the journey.

As I wrapped up the section I called "Woman to Woman" in the conclusion of *Earn Your Seat on a Corporate Board*, I sensed there was more to say on women and leadership. And for good reason!

Consider this, for example. Findings from two new analyses of data related to earnings and retirement "provide the most comprehensive look yet at women's career paths." Because many women made decisions when they were younger to get a higher education and build a career, they are now "in jobs that are more fulfilling, and they stay with them." And, those women "who enjoyed their jobs earlier in life were employed longer, independent of their education or earnings."[*] That translates into more opportunities to go far and lead others in your chosen field!

In researching *Women Make Great Leaders*, I discovered a wondrous group of high-profile women who are going places and making great contributions to our world. A few of the women I knew, but many I merely reached out to and they graciously agreed to be interviewed. (Unless I note otherwise, I had those conversations between July and December 2016.)

---

*Claire Cain Miller, "More Women in Their 60s and 70s Are Having 'Way Too Much Fun' to Retire," *NYTimes* online, "The Upshot," February 11, 2017.

I spoke to Baby Boomers (my generation), Baby Busters (or Gen-Xers, born between 1965 and 1979), and women of Gen Next (or Gen-Yers or Millennials, born between 1980 and 1995). Within each group are many stellar women who have made it to the top of their professions. Early on, they heard the whispers, the inner call to leadership. They answered this calling, and continue to answer it, with fierce passion and purpose—and the courage, boldness, and resilience required to attain the next level of leadership, and the next, and the next.

The truth can't be sugarcoated, though. These women—like you—faced and continue to face numerous challenges in every office where they've ever served. To help you appreciate what great women leaders are up against, I've included a description of the state of the union that is the backdrop against which you should read this book.

WOMEN ARE RISING SLOWLY, BUT MOMENTUM IS BUILDING

Growing up, I would occasionally be called by my mother to a "family meeting." My sister and I would join her at our kitchen table and Mom would announce what was about to change and our roles in it. These meetings taught me some early lessons about how to look at "news."

Consider this chapter something of a "family meeting." Imagine yourself sitting with your leadership "sisters" as I'm preparing to tell you about some changes taking place—and, possibly, the roles you'll play in them.

FIRST, THE NOT-SO-GOOD NEWS

In the last decade, more and more women leaders have emerged, but slowly. Released in September 2016, the Women in the Workplace study—a joint undertaking by LeanIn.org and McKinsey&Company—confirms what underlies the slow rise.

Here's a brief summary of the findings. (Visit womenin-theworkplace.com for links to the complete report.)

- Very few women are in line to become CEO: By the time women reach the senior VP level, they hold just 20 percent of line roles, and it's line roles that lead more directly to a C-suite office. (For example, in 2015, 90 percent of new CEOs in the S&P 500 were promoted or hired from line roles.)
- The pipeline problem: Women aren't just outside the pipeline to a top job; they are underrepresented at every level in most U.S. corporations. This disparity is especially noticeable among women of color, who face the most obstacles to advancement and who experience the "steepest drop-offs with seniority."
- The first promotion: Women are promoted more slowly than men are. This is most pronounced at the first step up, from entry level to manager, where the largest numbers of employees are involved.
- Limited access to leadership: Although most survey takers viewed sponsorship by a senior leader as a top factor in accelerating a person's advancement, access to input from senior management is less common for women than it is for men. And—no surprises here—that gap widens as men and women move through the promotion pipeline.

xvi WOMEN MAKE GREAT LEADERS

- Women ask for feedback, but are less likely to get it: Despite asking for informal feedback as often as men do, women report that they receive it less frequently. And, though managers say they rarely hesitate to give difficult feedback to women and men alike, female survey participants disclosed that they rarely receive it.
- Pushback during negotiations: Women who negotiate for a promotion or a compensation increase are negotiating at the same rates as men are. Yet, those same women are 30 percent more likely than their male counterparts to receive feedback that they are being "bossy," "too aggressive," or "intimidating" in their negotiating efforts.

Don't be disheartened, however. Think of the LeanIn.org and McKinsey study as a gift of insight. It provides you with a crystal-clear picture of the current landscape and tough terrain you may encounter as you make your moves to go as far and high and wide as your ambition can take you.

And that's a good thing! As the late-sixteenth-century proverb teaches, "Forewarned is forearmed."

Equal Work?

Data from the Pew Research Center reveal that the "share of women in the workforce has grown dramatically in recent decades and is expected to hit 47.1% in 2025." The flip side of that coin, however, is the prediction that by 2060 the percentage of women in the workplace will drop "to 46.3%."

WELCOME TO BECOMING!   xvii

Factors underlying that anticipated decline range from an aging population and more women deciding to retire to more mothers of young children—"especially moms with less education"—choosing not to work because child care is so expensive. Some sociologists even forecast a "reversion to traditional gender roles" as one potential cause of that reduction in women workers. Offsetting those dispiriting statistics, though, is the revelation that more "single women are withdrawing from the labor force in favor of attending school."[**]

Everyone who supports the idea and the ideal of women attaining equality in the workplace needs to redouble their efforts, because the country—in particular our economy health—will benefit from a large and diverse labor force.

NOW, THE BETTER NEWS

To counter the hard truth of those Women in the Workplace numbers, here's an encouraging word about diversity and open-mindedness.

McKinsey&Company's independent survey on that very subject offers this encouraging word: "We live in a deeply connected and global world… [in which] more diverse companies and institutions are achieving better performance. Most organizations… must do more to take full advantage of the opportunity that diverse leadership teams represent."[***] (The full Diversity Matters report is available at www.mckinsey.com.)

In other words (the operative ones being "better performance"), corporate America has had its eyes opened to the reality that having a greater share of women and a more representational

[**]Kristen Bellstrom, "Everyone's talking," Fortune online, "The Broadsheet," February 1, 2017.
[***]Vivian Hunt, Dennis Layton, and Sara Prince, "Why Diversity Matters," McKinsey&Company online, January 2015.

ethnic and racial mix at all levels of a company—in particular the top level, its leaders—translates to higher profits. CEOs nationwide will do well to devote time, energy, and dollars to recruiting, professionally developing, mentoring, and retaining talented women to secure a next generation of senior leadership.

Audi of America—"Committed to equal pay for equal work. Progress is for everyone."

One example of a business that has its eyes wide open is Audi. The luxury automobile manufacturer flexed its muscle by addressing "one of the most significant social issues of today" in its so-called daughter ad that championed gender equality in the workplace. Run during the third quarter of Super Bowl LI, female director Aoife McArdle's TV commercial nearly eclipsed the Patriots' triumphant comeback.

More than underscoring the message that girls can be equal to or better than boys (the daughter wins the modern equivalent of a soapbox derby), the message focuses on what will happen when those children become adults and vie for jobs in the workplace.

The father grapples with what he should tell his daughter. "That her dad is worth more than her mom? That despite her education, drive, skills, [and] intelligence, she will automatically be valued as less than every man she ever meets?" After a pregnant pause, he concludes that maybe he'll be able to tell her "something different."****

A toast to you, Ms. McArdle, and Audi!

The women you'll read about in these pages continually polish their talent with a capacity to work really hard, help others succeed, and play the game with fairness and honesty, with kindness and generosity. They never lose sight that their purpose is to dare boldly to make the world a better place.

These women are doers and risk takers. They face their fears head-on. When they misstep, they pick themselves up and use the lesson to inform their steps forward. Along the way, they are patient with the ebb and flow of life. Many become devoted wives, partners, and mothers while building careers and influence. They all remain true to their "work" as leaders in the world, carrying it out with the grace, diplomacy, and fortitude it requires.

> "I believe we [women] have made significant [progress] over the last several years... the increasing number of women in Congress, on corporate boards, in senior-level positions, starting businesses, and more. I believe now, more than ever, we have to capitalize on this momentum around female advocacy."
>
> —Karen Quintos, Chief Customer Officer, Dell

In sharing their stories, these women are cheering you on.

As for me, this book is one small way to send the elevator back down. I'd like you to consider these lessons the "greatest hits" of what I've learned. I've taken care to keep them pithy and a breeze to read. You can move through them one after another, or you can skip directly to a topic that interests you. Bottom line? I'm glad to have you on this learning journey with me!

FIND YOUR PASSION AND PURPOSE

"Trust to that prompting within you."
—Ralph Waldo Emerson

Passion and purpose are like two bookends. You need both to succeed.

Did you find your passion and purpose early? Or are you still seeking it? Either way, you are doing okay; the important thing is to be passionate about *something*.

For me, some big clues about my passion and purpose came early simply because I followed my curiosity.

Like many small towns in the 1960s, my hometown of Marshville, North Carolina, boasted a thriving business district made up of mom-and-pop stores. (Think the fictional Mayberry in the 1960s'-vintage sitcom *The Andy Griffith Show*.) Audrey's Dress Shop, Gaddy's Shoe Store, Creech's Five and Dime, The Fabric Shop, Rollins Jewelry Store, and Pfeiffer Hardware were a few of the shops owned and operated by locals.

Those shops were only a ten-minute walk from my neighborhood, and when I was a grade-schooler, they became my playground. I would visit them as often as possible, inquisitively making my "rounds" to check out what was new.

As humble as they were, with their counters, shelves, and racks of merchandise, these stores never failed to fascinate me.

And I also began to notice a lot about the shopping experiences these merchants delivered: I studied what they featured in their windows. I found myself touching the finishes and fabrics of their store's offerings. I took note of the store's natural light (or lack of it). I was mindful of whether the front doors opened to the ring of a bell affixed to the inside knob to alert the shopkeeper someone had entered.

Your Passion Can Get You Hired

When asked how he goes about interviewing and choosing which candidate to hire, Victor Ho, CEO of FiveStars, a customer loyalty network for small businesses, has this to say: "I want to figure why you work and what your deeper purposes are… I want to see if the person has thought on a very deep level about why they dedicate such a big portion of their life to what they do."*

A word to the wise. Come at the subject of what you're passionate about, what purpose underpins what you do. Prepare and polish your answers to as many variations on those themes as you can imagine. If the interviewer doesn't pose them, take the initiative and do so yourself—and take first place among the candidates!

Of special interest to me was whether someone was on hand to greet me. Were they warm and welcoming even though I was a kid? Or were they dismissive? In one store that catered to children, I was closely watched. Because I was unaccompanied by a parent, they probably thought I would shoplift. (It was naughty fun when

---

*Adam Bryant, "Victor Ho of FiveStars: Take Management Advice from Interns," *NYTimes online*, "Corner Office," September 23, 2016.

a group of us would enter together and purposely spread out all over the store. It drove the storekeeper bonkers!)

This early curiosity made my choice to earn a business degree in college a natural one, and to follow it immediately with an MBA. Upon graduation, I joined the brand management department of R.J. Reynolds Tobacco Company, where I got great schooling in how and what customers buy. And that experience also solidified an understanding of why customers buy, which enabled me to write a customer loyalty book that was named on Harvard's list of "Working Knowledge" titles.

And, in case you're wondering, I am *still* a recreational shopper!

MOVE TOWARD WHAT INTERESTS YOU

Don't feel anxious if, unlike me, you're still fuzzy about your ultimate career direction. In fact, your life will be far richer if you experiment with a variety of jobs, roles, and functions. That way you can zoom in on your purpose and passion. That's because interests are not just discovered, they can also be developed. Angela Duckworth explores this principle in her book, *Grit: The Power of Passion and Perseverance.* For example, she cites that Julia Child didn't fall in love with French cuisine until she was in her late thirties.

Early jobs are often trial-and-error processes that reveal what you *don't want.*

It's analogous to having an annual eye exam. When the optometrist shows you images of different-sized letters and asks, "Is it clearer with A or B?" your answers help narrow down the prescription that is right for you.

Likewise, Duckworth advises that in making career and job choices, always move in a direction that feels better than worse.

Shirley Ann Jackson, president of Rensselaer Polytechnic Institute, offers a similar opinion. "You start out on a trajectory, a direction. But you have to understand that there are a lot of forces along the way that can change your trajectory. But you try to keep your eye on that North Star and understand why you started down the path in the first place."[**]

> "I confess it took a fair bit of job swapping before I knew that psychological research would become my long-term career. But in each of those jobs, I picked up knowledge and skills that I was able to weave into my current work."
>
> —Angela Duckworth, MacArthur Fellow and professor of psychology at the University of Pennsylvania

Here's how one of my interviewees discovered her passion in a high school biology lab, and how it's fed her purpose in the world.

HOW DR. IMOGEN COE FOUND HER PASSION AND PURPOSE

Dean of the Faculty of Science at Toronto's Ryerson University, Dr. Imogen Coe has a keen sense of passion. As she discussed in our interview, once she discovered her love of and dedication to science, it propelled her to lead courageously.

Born in the United Kingdom into a family of modest means, her parents taught the importance of "fairness" and that "every man/woman" deserved a chance. Dr. Coe absorbed the values

---

** Adam Bryant, "Shirley Ann Jackson: Keep Your Eye on the North Star," NYTimes online, "Corner Office," May 27, 2016.

of equity, diversity, and inclusivity, and they are at the core of everything she undertakes.

Education was the priority. The youngest of four siblings, she attended an all-girls school and always had a keen curiosity of the natural world. She recalls that one of her very first questions was, "How do bugs *work*?"

When I asked her to tell me when she first fell in love with science, she said with a chuckle: "My high school biology class, when I dissected a worm. While other girls considered the task 'gross,' I was struck by the magic and beauty of the worm's nerve cord."

> "In order to lead an organization, you have to be incredibly comfortable in your own skin, and the only way to do that is to be confident in who you are."
>
> —Gracia Martore, president and CEO of Tegna Inc. and former CEO of Gannett Company

That passion for science led her to earn a PhD in biology, but soon thereafter she found that making her way as a woman in academia would also take courage and perseverance. The field was full of highly competitive men who were natural self-promoters. Teamwork was not always on their radar screen. Early on when she voiced her opinions, people declared her to be "outspoken." But she didn't buy it. "No," she said, "I'm just *spoken*."

Around the age of forty, Dr. Coe reports, "I reached a high level of academic leadership, which enabled me to start changing the culture around me to one that was more collaborative and team based."

Here are some things she learned:

- Leadership is about building "social capital." To empower people, they must feel heard and their contributions appreciated. Leaders must encourage their team members to go outside of their comfort zones.

- Leaders need to have champions too. She defines them as, "Those people who are behind me, holding me up, pushing me forward at my own pace."
- As a leader, you must get out of your peoples' way so they can innovate.
- Active listening—concentrating on and grasping the other person's words, responding empathetically, and remembering the outcome—is hugely important.
- When you make a misstep as a leader, own it and learn from it. In the process, be kind to yourself and forgive yourself. Remind yourself that you're doing your best.
- Young fathers need parental leave too. They need to get out of the lab and help with the new baby.
- Women in science need to learn how important and strategic it is to build a large, strong network of colleagues. Staying in the lab with your head down doesn't cut it.
- The drive for equity and diversity in science must be led from the top. In this cause, influential and supportive male allies are needed to promote the equity and diversity agenda.

Today Dr. Coe is firmly anchored in her purpose of advancing women's leadership in the STEM disciplines—science, technology, engineering, and mathematics—and is a frequent speaker on the topic. Her track record and that of her female colleagues prove that women are essential to the sciences and have much to contribute to the field.

Mom's Sage Advice

My mom, Mildred Marsh Griffin, frequently said to me, "Rome wasn't built in a day." That advice helped me endure long dry spells. For instance, it took me seven years to get my first book, *Customer Loyalty: How to Earn It, How to Keep It*, published. But the setbacks were key learning moments. And, ultimately, the book opened doors for me that I never could have imagined.

Don't Bend to Expectations

Years ago, a male colleague confided in me that his dad spent his career in human resources and encouraged him to do the same. As a dutiful son, he complied, but it was not a good fit; he felt unfulfilled most of the time. My colleague stuck it out for more than a decade, and only after his dad died did he feel he was free to try something new.

Remember: This is your life. Don't bend to another person's expectations. Be courageous and find your own path. Be true to your passion and purpose. Throughout your career, repeat this inspiring adage to encourage your every move: "Self-confidence can ebb and flow, but self-belief never falters."

TAKEAWAYS

- Passion, purpose, hard work, and perseverance—all are essential to you becoming an outstanding leader.
- One of life's joys is remembering when you first fell in love with your calling.
- Tying your passion and purpose to your life's work is a powerful career accelerant.

- When you are confronted with inevitable career setbacks and disappointments, it helps to remind yourself of your purpose. Purpose gets you up and going again.
- It takes determination and self-confidence to keep on the trail to find your passion. Don't expect a lightning bolt. Instead, think of it as a journey toward what feels better and away from what feels worse.

AIM HIGH

*"When you reach for the stars you may not quite get one,
but you won't come up with a handful of mud either."*
—Leo Burnett

Men have been conditioned to aim high. Not so much women. That's why my heart sang when, during our conversation, I asked technology leader Karen Rogge for advice for middle managers wanting to move forward in their careers, and she said simply, "Aim high."

> While it may take some time to achieve a C-level or board position, if you set your sights on this goal today, the odds are greater that you will achieve your goal. Once you have a long-term C-level goal in mind, it will begin to influence all aspects of your thought process, such as taking a routine analysis beyond just the numbers and anticipating next steps for the business, or broadening your perspective on potential career moves, etc.

From humble beginnings, growing up on a farm in California (started by her Italian immigrant grandfather), Rogge learned, in her words, "The values of hard work, persistence, independent thought, and honoring commitments." Those values were key to Rogge's vision and perseverance to gain the skill sets required to eventually reach an executive position. Here's how she did it.

During her career, she moved through a progression of increasingly responsible financial analyst and managerial roles across many businesses within Hewlett-Packard (HP). Rogge's first major step up was to head the finance function for an HP business division as a "Division Controller," leading a team of 150 people and reporting directly to the general manager.

After a few tours in that role for different businesses within the HP network, she was looking for a change—and accepted the challenge to lead the transformation of the information technology (IT) function for a $4-billion HP business, with 500 people located across twelve countries.

> "Work is not graded on a curve. There is no partial credit for using the correct methodology but doing the math incorrectly. A decimal in the wrong place is deadly in business."
>
> —Melissa Brown Herkt, civil engineer

While Rogge enjoyed the IT world, she strategically understood she needed experience at "the heart of the business" and closer to the end customer. By leveraging her IT background, she shifted career paths and moved into general management positions, leading software businesses—initially at HP and later as a VP and general manager at Inktomi.

Rogge's next major career shift occurred as she accepted the broadly defined "VP of Corporate Finance, Treasurer & Principal Accounting Officer" role for Seagate Technology, a $9-billion storage technology company. This was a period of tumultuous change at Seagate as the company grew rapidly through the introduction of new products, expanded into new markets, and successfully completed key acquisitions. This experience laid the groundwork for her move into Seagate's C-Suite and the boardroom. As she put it, "This experience rounded out my background. I now had a broad perspective into the day-to-day workings of a global company across the corporate level, the businesses unit level, as well as multiple business functions."

In her next role, Rogge was looking to leverage her broad finance and operations management background as well as to have an impact at both the strategic and the operational levels of the business. Rogge's next move was into the CFO role for a $300-million public technology company, Extreme Networks.

Mom's Sage Advice

Cecile Richards is the president of Planned Parenthood and daughter of former Texas governor Ann Richards. Reflecting on what her mom's best piece of advice was, Cecile remembers her always saying that "the answer to life was YES. She believed in taking every opportunity that came your way—new job, new challenge—particularly for women, who often second-guess themselves. She never regretted the mistakes she made, only the chances she never took." Cecile often heard her mother admonish her to "quit worrying and just do it," advice she puts into practice every day.

More recently, Karen Rogge has achieved her "aim high" prize by leveraging her unique blend of financial operations and general management background, as well as strategic and operational skills, to create the RYN Group, a management consulting firm that provides CFO and strategic advisory services for public and private companies. Clients engage her services to work closely with the CEO and senior team to focus the company's strategy for growth and improve the company's financial and operational performance. In addition, she is an independent board director for Alliance Partners360, a pharmaceutical company focused on women's health, and an Audit Committee member for the Ronald McDonald House at Stanford.

Make no mistake about it, there's a real connection between achieving your aim-high prize and happiness, which the study conducted by Cecile K. Cho that follows shows definitively.

Happiness = Achieving High Goals

Back in 2011 University of California-Riverside professor Cecile K. Cho set up two experiments to compare people who set ambitious goals with those who set conservative ones. One experiment had participants choose stocks; the other had them solve puzzles.

When Professor Cho measured the satisfaction level of the participants with the goals they had achieved, she found that those who "set high goals for themselves" are "happier in the long run."

That result corresponds to and validates research on personal and professional goal-setting that social psychologist Heidi G. Halvorson, PhD, conducted (I recommend that you add her book *Succeed: How We Can Reach Our Goals* to your recommended reading list as you set goals for your own career.) "It's about stretching yourself and aiming high, while still hanging on to a bit of realism. That's going to give you the most satisfaction, the most bang for your goal-setting buck."

Or, as Professor Cho put it succinctly, "The moral of the story is don't sell yourself short. Aim high."*

AIM HIGH ACADEMICALLY TOO

Dr. Pamela McCauley is a professor in the Department of Industrial Engineering and Management Systems at the University of

---

*Courtney Rubin, "The Route to Happiness: Set ambitious goals, says a study," Wire, Inc. online, August 23, 2011.

Central Florida in Orlando. (You'll read more about this remarkable leader in Lesson #8—Find Your People.)

In our interview, Dr. McCauley talked about the profound impact that sitting in on a lecture by Howard G. Adams, PhD, during her sophomore year in college had on her self-belief. She had never met an African-American man who had earned a doctorate, nor did she know such an advanced degree was even possible. She and a friend went up to him afterward and eagerly asked, "Do you think we could get our PhD degrees?" He replied, "Of course you can!" That was a pivotal moment for young McCauley. Those four powerful words set the stage for her to pursue her own doctorate. She went on to become the first African-American woman in her home state of Oklahoma to earn that degree.

BEWARE OF IMPOSTOR SYNDROME

Sometimes aiming high brings the baggage of "Impostor Syndrome," a term coined by clinical psychologists Pauline Rose Clance and Suzanne Imes in 1978. The phenomenon is seen among people—many of them high-achievers—who feel "their success has been due to some mysterious fluke or luck or great effort; they are afraid their achievements are due to 'breaks' and not the result of their own ability and competence" (paulineroseclance.com/impostor_phenomenon.html). This, even though others looking at their achievements from the outside would say they were successful.

How to Become a CEO

In 2010 Beth Mooney made history when she was named as CEO of KeyCorp and thus became the first woman to hold that title at a top-20 U.S. bank. She hadn't aimed that high when she began her career in banking. But she was self-reflective, and as she took on more and more responsibility at different levels in the industry, she started to look in the mirror and think that that top spot might just be within reach.

Just as she herself experienced, Mooney offers this advice to women (and men) who will get opportunities to lead as they pursue their ambitions:

• Take a tough job… outside your comfort zone so people… realize… you're scalable, nimble, and… [adaptable in] new situations.
• Never stop investing in your own abilities and… learning.

As a leader, Mooney has always taken constructive criticism to heart and has made a point of working well within teams. As a corporate leader, she doesn't focus on differences; rather, her intent is to bring out the best in others so that the corporation succeeds as a whole.**

Applying this to a work setting, the Impostor Syndrome sometimes manifests itself in a feeling that you don't belong in the great job you've been chosen for. I had a bad case of it both in graduate school and in my first job. I longed for a soothing inner voice to whisper, "I've got your back"; instead, believing I was a fraud, I incessantly said to myself, "You're not good enough, and any moment the boss and your colleagues will find out and the consequences will be severe."

** Gregory Jones, "The View from KeyCorp CEO Beth Mooney's Office atop Key Tower," Smart Business Cleveland online, June 1, 2013.

Facebook COO Sheryl Sandberg shined a spotlight on the term in her bestselling book *Lean In,* admitting that she felt like an impostor as a Harvard student and later in the corporate world.

What to do? Here are some quick thoughts to help you manage your feelings—but ultimately, you might want to seek a counselor who understands IP. That professional can help you with coping tools.

Know that you're not alone—and no one is immune.

Talk with others about the issue; find a mentor who relates.

Don't buy into negative self-talk; make it positive only, please.

Keep track of your accomplishments and remind yourself about them often.

AIM HIGH SUCCESS TIPS

1. To excel in anything, first look inward and consider your values. Honesty, kindness, perseverance, and humility are cornerstones to success.

2. Adversity is a great teacher. When the hard knocks come your way, journal what you are feeling and learning. These lessons are the "bread crumbs" that will lead to your house of success.

3. Trust yourself more.

4. Choose your inner circle of friends who will champion you in good times and bad. That's critical to confidently and joyfully making it through life. Look for people who are honest and will be kind to you. Be there for them, and hope they will be there for you.

5. Relax more and enjoy the ride. I can see now, from

the vantage point of a long and fascinating career, that serendipity and synchronicity are embedded in the universe and those forces always have our back.

TAKEAWAYS

- In any career, it requires courage, passion, hard work, and perseverance to truly "Aim High."
- It takes vision and a savvy understanding of business to put yourself on a C-suite track early, as Rogge did.
- You may need to "wander around" a bit in various levels and areas of responsibility to sharpen your definition of how to "Aim High." As your career grows and success ensues, don't hesitate to amend your definition.
- You can be hardwired for Imposter Syndrome. A good counselor can help you successfully deal with it.

LEAVE NO STONE UNTURNED

"When you get into a tight place and everything goes against you… never give up then, for that is just the place and time that the tide will turn."
—Harriet Beecher Stowe

Directors and Boards magazine named Sheila Hooda as a "Director to Watch 2016." That's a huge recognition in its own right, but it is especially remarkable when you learn about Hooda's life story, as I did in our conversation.

A native of Pune, in Western India, Hooda is the eldest of four children. The close-knit family lived peaceably until Hooda's father unexpectedly passed away shortly before her eleventh birthday. Her mother was now a young widow, and Hooda stepped in to become her right hand, attending community meetings and helping to raise her younger siblings. Hooda wanted to set an example and be a role model for them. She had always been driven and now, even more, dedicated herself to achieving excellence by working harder than her peers, always seeking to do more than was expected of her. She had to be self-reliant and leave absolutely nothing to chance!

Hooda attended what now is the University of Pune—the best undergraduate school in her region—and she graduated with an honors degree in mathematics. Although undecided about her career path, she resolved to find a position where she could make a considerable impact and achieve her highest aspirations. Leaving no stone unturned, Hooda applied to a graduate school nearly 600 miles from home: the prestigious Indian Institute of Management, where less than 1 percent of applicants are accepted.

At the time, women made up less than 10 percent of the student population; Hooda was one of only twelve female students in her class. Acceptance (and thereafter completing the institute's Post Graduate Diploma in Management) was her first big breakout moment. (She says with a smile in her voice that she also met her future husband two weeks into the semester!)

She began her career at American Express Bank in India, and in the late 1980s, Hooda and her husband immigrated to the United States. Both were well-schooled in English: Her husband was accepted into the PhD program at the University of Chicago, and she earned a spot in the MBA program there.

Again, doing everything possible to achieve her goals, Hooda applied and was chosen for a super-selective summer internship with world-renowned McKinsey&Company. Hooda was the only candidate from Chicago's Booth Business School selected that year to intern in the U.S. Another breakout moment she grabbed with pride and gratitude.

"What did you wear to the interview?" I asked.

"I bought a pair of shoes at Payless Shoes for $10 and went to the Salvation Army store and found an appropriate suit for $15," she proudly shared.

Briefcase "Essentials" from a Woman Who's Been Caught Without

Thinking about Hooda's need to be both resourceful and clever as she went about finding clothes that gave her the professional look required for her interview makes me think of some essential "notions" I always have with me in a set of cosmetics bags in my briefcase. You never know when you're going to need:

- Cosmetics
    - Lipstick (plus a straw to keep your lipstick intact)
    - Compact (with a mirror is best)
    - Dental floss (plus a good friend who will tell you if you have spinach stuck between your teeth!)
    - Nail file
    - Small scissors
    - Hand lotion
    - Wet wipes
    - Tissues
- Meeting Miscellany
    - Calendar (I'm old-fashioned; I also carry a paper calendar because I need to "see" what's on my docket.)
    - Pen and notepaper
    - Case with your business cards
    - Cell phone
    - Portable charger
    - Ear pods
    - Agenda
    - Address book (for those contacts not in my phone)
    - Collapsible umbrella (mini is best)
- Energy Kit
    - Water
    - Protein bar

- Trail mix
- Breath mints
- Vitamins (B_{12} and magnesium both help you stay calm and clear-minded in stressful moments)

Over the summer, Hooda impressed McKinsey with her dedication, initiative, and smarts. McKinsey even paid the tuition for her second year at Booth, provided she returned to them upon graduation. Under that stone was yet another breakout moment!

The Only Move That Matters Is Your Next One

People with successful careers don't "climb the corporate ladder" anymore. That's what Google's former career coach and cofounder of the company's career mentoring program Jenny Blake says in her newly released *PIVOT: The Only Move That Matters Is Your Next One*. In an economy where workers and their employers are less loyal to each other, talk of moving up the rungs of a career ladder is outdated. Why? Because it doesn't account for the various lateral moves that many professionals can make between job positions, projects, and even companies that result in them feeling more fulfilled.

To help you find more happiness at work or from your next professional move, Blake urges you to think of your career in a different way. "Consider your career like a smartphone, not a ladder. It's up to you to 'download apps' for different skills, interests, and side projects that sound interesting and fulfilling to you."

These downloadable apps take many shapes: They can be classes you take to acquire skills or a language you've always wanted to learn, or they can be new activities like joining an office book club or volunteering to help with a company-sponsored com-munity project. Virtually anything that excites and motivates you helps you grow as a person and, by extension, become a highly sought-after employee.

You're much more likely to get hired for the unique skills you have—whether those come from inside or outside the office, Blake says. In fact, having different outside hobbies and interests not only boosts your productivity and work, it also helps you deal with a job you dislike.

Although her advice is particularly germane for recent graduates, who place a lot of emphasis on their first job out of college, it's nonetheless relevant to all professionals. "Any job you take will give you 'apps' that will help [you] improve time management, communication, money management." Those skills will better equip you for your own next change or, shall we say, "upgrade."

Whether you're a Baby Boomer or a Millennial, you'd do well to get a print or e-book version of *PIVOT: The Only Move That Matters Is Your Next One* and start taking your own notes.

Armed with her MBA and work history at McKinsey, Hooda joined Wall Street and made a significant mark as managing direc-tor, global equities, in the Investment Banking Division at Credit Suisse Group, and in strategy, M&A, and corporate development roles at TIAA, the retirement and asset management company. She also started and provided guidance for several diversity and leadership initiatives and served on multiple nonprofit boards focused on education and women's empowerment. In a 2010, issue of the *Financial Times* publication for board members "Agenda," Hooda was honored in their inaugural "Diversity 100" top board candidates list. In addition, she was invited to join the prestigious Council on Foreign Relations.

A lifelong practice of leaving no stone unturned led Hooda ultimately to found her own company, Alpha Advisory Partners, in 2013, where she has served as its CEO and president, focusing on strategy and long-term planning. The firm advises on strategic positioning, mergers and acquisitions, turnaround and transformation, and customer-centricity and digital business models for companies in the financial and business services sectors. Prior to founding Alpha Advisory Partners, Hooda served as the global head of strategy and business development in the Investors Segment of Thomson Reuters' Financial & Risk business group.

> "When I stand before God at the end of my life, I would hope that I would not have a single bit of talent left, and I could say, 'I used everything you gave me.'"
>
> —Erma Bombeck

"Sheila brings significant experience in the asset management industry from her senior roles in strategy and business development across a number of global organizations as well as her service on corporate boards," says George R. Aylward, president and chief executive officer of Virtus Investment Partners Board. "We welcome… her [to] our board and we look forward to benefiting from her experience and insights."[*]

In addition, she serves on the board of directors of Mutual of Omaha Insurance Company—a Fortune 400 company—where she is a member of the Investment Committee and the Risk Committee. Hooda has also been recognized by the National Association of Corporate Directors as a Board Leadership Fellow.

Her advice for women with high aspirations includes:

---

[*] "Sheila Hooda Joins Virtus Investment Partners Board," December 12, 2016, "Investor Relations" online news.

1. Leave no stone unturned.

2. Focus on soft skills. Learn the art of balancing smarts, grit, and ambition with elegance and femininity.

3. Have true faith and confidence in yourself. At the end of the day, each one of us has the power to lead the kind of life we aspire to.

4. Take the time to give back and leave the world a better place.

Do You Count Yourself a Mentally Strong Woman?

In her *Wall Street Journal* best seller, *13 Things Mentally Strong People Don't Do*, Amy Morin, LCSW, outlines behaviors, traits, and attitudes that characterize women who lead from a position of mental strength. Here are snapshots of a handful of those qualities that you'll want to test yourself against.

- **They Don't Give Away Their Power:** They don't allow others to control them, and they don't give someone else power over them. They don't say things like, "My boss makes me feel bad" because they understand that they are in control over their own emotions and they have a choice in how they respond.

- **They Don't Waste Energy on Things They Can't Control:** You won't hear a mentally strong person complaining over lost luggage or traffic jams. Instead, they focus on what they can control in their lives. They recognize that sometimes, the only thing they can control is their attitude.

- **They Don't Fear Taking Calculated Risks:** They don't take reckless or foolish risks, but they don't mind taking calculated risks. Mentally strong people spend time weighing the risks and benefits before making a big decision, and they're fully informed of the potential downsides before they take action.

- **They Don't Fear Alone Time:** Mentally strong people can tolerate being alone and they don't fear silence. They aren't afraid to be alone with their thoughts and they can use downtime to be productive. They enjoy their own company and aren't dependent on others for companionship and entertainment all the time but instead can be happy alone.

- **They Don't Feel the World Owes Them Anything:** They don't feel entitled to things in life. They weren't born with a mentality that others would take care of them or that the world must give them something. Instead, they look for opportunities based on their own merits.

- **They Don't Expect Immediate Results:** Whether they are working on improving their health or getting a new business off the ground, mentally strong people don't expect immediate results. Instead, they apply their skills and time to the best of their ability and understand that real change takes time.

I strongly encourage you to get a copy of Morin's *13 Things Mentally Strong People Don't Do: Take Back Your Power, Embrace Change, Face Your Fears, and Train Your Brain for Happiness and Success* and underline, highlight, or circle still more of her empowering observations that you can aspire to grow into and make your own.

TAKEAWAYS

- Hooda models the classic immigrant mentality. She and her husband saw America as rife with possibility and leveraged that possibility into opportunity.

Here are McGill's tips for going as far as your ambitions can take you:

- The merger brought with it tremendous change, and with change always comes opportunity. So, if things are in flux in your firm, look for ways to leverage yourself into more accountability.
- More accountability comes with the risk of failure. Be willing to put yourself on the line.
- In times of change, express yourself confidently and boldly in meetings with top executives. Voice your commitment to the organization and your interest in growing professionally.
- Earn people's trust. It's the foundation of anyone's reputation in both life and work. The first step I took in earning people's trust was to learn the name of anyone who worked in my space—and to use it each and every time we interacted.

KIM WYANT

One game into the New York University (NYU) 2015 men's soccer team season, Kim Wyant received an unexpected call from the university's associate athletic director. A crisis had arisen. Wyant was told the team's coach had stepped down… and she was being invited by the selection committee—the athletic director, two associate athletic directors, and a university vice president—to take over the program. Saying yes would make her "the first and only woman to lead a men's National Collegiate Athletic Association (NCAA) soccer program."

To the Manner Born

When I asked about her childhood, Wyant giggled when she told me that growing up in Miami, Florida, her ambition was to be a wide receiver for the Miami Dolphins. One Christmas she received a Dolphins replica jersey, which she wore religiously, surrendering it only when her mother demanded it for the occasional wash.

Wyant was an independent kid who earned her own money with a paper route and odd jobs throughout the neighborhood. And her childhood years were filled with sports. She hung with the boys, riding her bike to the park for all kinds of athletic activities.

One fateful afternoon, the baseball team was forming up in the park and the parent in charge told Wyant she couldn't play because she was a girl. Surprised and perplexed, she biked home to share the news.

"Gather your things," her willful mom told her.

Wyant shared, "And so we peeled out of driveway down to the park. My mom marched up to the male organizer. 'My daughter plays or I will sue you for discrimination.' That moment of watching my mom stand up for me was very empowering."

Suffice it to say, Wyant was immediately welcomed to the team.

Once out of college, she chose internal and external sales— roles that allowed her to control her own schedule and accommodate her participation in sports.

Later on, while still playing on the USA Women's national teams, Wyant's devotion for soccer led her to start clinics and camps where she taught young people her beloved sport. This soon turned into such a prosperous small business that she was able to buy a house in her mid-20s.

During our chat, Wyant remembered that phone call well. "It was a defining moment of my career. Absorbing the news, I found the situation both scary and intriguing. Scary in the sense of concern for the well-being of the coach who departed; was he okay? And scary for the team and the apprehension they must be feeling about this abrupt change. But I was also intrigued. It was instantly clear to me that this was a *once-in-a-lifetime opportunity*, for which I had been preparing all my life."

Wyant, a mother of two daughters, then seven and nine, was ready to make the transition back to work. Her prior experience had included a stint as head coach of the women's soccer teams at Florida Atlantic University and Dowling College, as well as head coach of the New York Athletic Club women's soccer team. In 2014 she had been interviewing for jobs. One she felt especially qualified for had gone on for three interviews. She was surprised when she was not selected.

But Wyant's instincts—both personally and professionally— told her that something bigger must be on its way.

Wyant came to NYU with a remarkable playing and coaching resume. As a player, she was the first goalkeeper in the history of the U.S. Women's National Soccer Team, appearing in the squad's inaugural game in Italy in 1985. In all, Wyant played sixteen games as the U.S. goalkeeper, recording the team's first-ever win and shutout. In 2008, she received the Special Recognition Award from the National Soccer Hall of Fame for her contributions to the National Team.

Yet, her acceptance to coach NYU's men's soccer team didn't come without some consternation. A sleepless night ensued. Wyant imagined the worst: a meeting where the team filed out in protest.

As she contemplated the opportunity with family and close friends, Wyant realized that the challenges and precedent were huge. With the job would come high visibility as a woman at the head of a men's team. The team was in distress. There would be added scrutiny, and many other first-time challenges would be on her plate. Was she up for it?

Her female coaching colleagues pointed out that male coaches (with lesser resumes) would likely leap at the opportunity!

In the final analysis, Wyant followed her heart. "I would rather fail trying than step away from the challenge. The selection committee was looking for the best candidate, and I was their first choice."

The rightness of the decision is reflected in the team's stats since she took over as coach at NYU. In the 2015 season, the team had 6 wins and 12 losses; in 2016 that improved to 9 wins, 2 ties, and 7 losses. In June 2016, the New York Surf Soccer Club welcomed Wyant both as a member of their coaching leadership team and a member of their board of directors.

Wyant's advice to women striving to lead includes the following ideas:

1. Be yourself.

2. Make the commitment to be the very best you can be in the leadership role you choose by continuing to educate yourself about best practices.

3. Be transparent, responsible, and accountable.

4. Own your mistakes.

5. Create a team culture where everyone understands their role. The more clarity on the role, the better the team.

6. Show appreciation for everyone with positive state-
   ments like "I appreciate your attitude." "I value
   you."

Learn a Business from the Ground Up

Being prepared when breakthrough opportunities come your
way is a convergence of many factors: your temperament, drive,
curiosity, education, work history, and can-do/will-do attitude.
Campbell Soup President and CEO Denise Morrison had known
since girlhood that she wanted to be a leader in business. "I
developed a strategic process for my career plan that set the final
destination, developed the career track, identified skills to build,
took line positions to gain experience, and sought leadership and
management training on the job, through special assignments,
coaching, and networking." Her aspirations played out right on
cue in the real world. For instance, her role as a marketing vice
president for Nestlé actually put her boots on the ground in a
manufacturing plant. That experience, she says, "[deepened my]
appreciation for how the supply chain works."*

DEIRDRE QUINN

Deirdre Quinn, CEO and cofounder of Lafayette 148, started her
fashion career at Liz Claiborne. Her first assignment was a basic
job in the pattern room. Soon thereafter, she was promoted to
secretary to the head of production. Her breakthrough moment
came when she was sitting in a meeting taking notes. The men at
the table were discussing that skirts were trending up that season,
and someone needed to go to Korea the next day to oversee the

*John Bussey, "How Women Can Get Ahead: Advice from Female CEOs," WSJ online, May 18, 2012.

shortening of 200,000 skirts. When nobody spoke up, Quinn said, "I'll go."

The next day she got on a plane to Korea, stayed in the country three months, and got the job done. From there on out, Quinn became the "go-to" person for getting problems solved. Assignments took her to places like El Salvador, Haiti, Sri Lanka, and India. By the time she was twenty-eight, she was leading a team as VP of operations.

Quinn's wisdom about how to succeed?

- Don't be late to meetings. If a meeting is to start at 9:00, and an attendee has yet to arrive, she closes the door.
- To help her in hiring the right people, she sometimes says during an interview, "Don't you hate getting up early in the morning?" If the interviewee answers, "I am so not a morning person," Quinn knows immediately that the person isn't the right fit. She wants to work with people who are happy in the morning. Period.
- Employees right out of college have to work especially hard and they need to have patience. Of course, a little luck helps too.
- You can learn from a bad boss just as much as you can from a good one.
- Don't be afraid to go the extra mile. Embrace your job every day.**

** Adam Bryant, "If a Meeting Starts at 9, Be There at 8," NYTimes online, "Corner Office," November 4, 2016.

TAKEAWAYS

- Learn people's names. (I'm terrible at this, and flub it constantly. I'm still a work in progress, though!) It truly is a first step in trust building.
- Times of change are rich with breakout opportunities. Seize the moment and leverage it while you can; these types of windows can close quickly.
- More accountability comes with risk of failure.
- Be willing to put yourself on the line.
- Seizing opportunity often means going outside of your comfort zone and taking risks. One way to deal with this discomfort is to ask yourself, what's the worst thing that can happen?
- Say yes to a messy, burdensome assignment no one else wants.
- Be clear about who does what so that each team member performs her best.
- Short, frequent affirmations—"Great job on that new design" or "Your positivity is contagious; thank you"—help to create a great workplace culture.

INSIST ON FEEDBACK

"There is no failure. Only feedback."
—Robert Allen

Gathering candid feedback about your work performance is crucial to earning your way to the next level. Getting routine and regular feedback from your boss is important.

But don't depend on your annual review! It's too little to late. You'll have plenty of big learning moments throughout the year. Take the initiative to meet with management to discuss your role and your performance to get the most from these critical learning opportunities.

USE DISAPPOINTMENTS TO LEARN AND EVOLVE

Whenever disappointments happen, ask for feedback. That's a key insight veteran business exec Jamie McDonald shared in our chat.

Google "Jamie McDonald" and you'll see that as founder of Generosity Inc., she's Baltimore's gift to raising funds for worthy causes. For years, however, she had worked hard to build her brand in the rough-and-tumble world of international investment banking.

"Tell Me One Thing I Don't Want to Hear"

Beth Comstock is vice chairman of General Electric and a member of Nike's board of directors. She's a strong advocate for keeping feedback at the office flowing in all directions.

She recognizes that the more senior a person is in her career, the less likely she is to hear the truth because subordinates are in the business of pleasing the boss. "They want to handle things so that they're not bringing you just the problems."

To counter that reality, Comstock has started saying to her direct reports, "Tell me one thing I don't want to hear. It's OK to give me some bad news. In fact, I want it."

Comstock contends that leaders need to view tension as a good thing and to go about using it to best effect. "If everybody on the team thinks something is good, it's probably not that good." By directly asking for bad news you identify a problem—or potential problem—and move forward together to resolve it—or head it off at the pass.*

McDonald's "heads-down" work style had speeded her climb during her early years with Deutsche Bank. But when she was passed over on her first nomination to managing director, McDonald asked for a meeting with her boss. "I understand that my partners feel I am not ready," she said. "Please give me some feedback."

Her boss's feedback changed McDonald's life. "He told me, 'Look, you are only twenty-nine years old. You're moving fast. It's time for you to pause. Look back down the mountain. [Start] recognizing and appreciating the many people who have contributed to your success.'"

---

* Adam Bryant, "Beth Comstock of General Electric: Granting Permission to Innovate," NYTimes online, "Corner Office," June 17, 2016.

His words resonated deeply with McDonald. They opened her eyes to the importance of bonding with her staff and colleagues, taking the time to understand their needs and to collaborate on projects and to help them perform well. As McDonald puts it, "I saw we are all in this together. No more heads down. I was now heads up!" A year later, she was awarded the promotion.

McDonald gleaned many more insights from her early days in the workplace, such as:

- Establish in your boss's mind the goal you have for yourself.
- Learn the art of being graciously assertive. I began my conversation with my boss saying, "I understand that my partners feel I am not ready…" That set a positive tone for what was a productive meeting.
- When you ask for feedback, be ready for what you hear.
- Don't limit feedback to just your boss. Your subordinates, peers, colleagues, and even your spouse or partner are great sources as well.

Women Leaders and Sports

McDonald loved playing team sports. She was on a field hockey team in high school and also took the only opening on the track team. Her small frame (5 feet 4 inches and a slight 120 pounds) didn't deter her from throwing the javelin and shot put!

Through those experiences McDonald learned that playing team sports in childhood, adolescence, and young adulthood helps women thrive in business, and it propels a lot of women to top corporate spots. Why? Because team sports teach you these basics, among others, that you'll want to hone if you're to succeed in the rough-and-tumble world of making deals.

- How to share roles and be flexible when you have to step in for a teammate
- How to work together toward a common goal
- How to develop thick skin emotionally (don't take it personally when the coach yells at you)
- How to push through even when you're tired or weak (exercised muscles grow stronger)
- How to assert yourself diplomatically (balance listening to coach's advice with stating your own assessment/opinion)
- Among many accomplished executives, here are four standout female leaders who played team sports:[**]
    - PepsiCo CEO Indra Nooyi. Her sport? Cricket, which she learned in her native India.
    - SEC Chairman Mary Schapiro. Her sports? Lacrosse and field hockey, which she played during undergraduate days at Franklin & Marshall College in Pennsylvania.
    - Kraft Foods CEO Irene Rosenfeld. Her sports? Or, rather, what *didn't* she play? She participated on four varsity teams in high school and she continued with basketball at Cornell.
    - Sunoco CEO Lynn Laverty Elsenhans. Her sport? She proudly played on Rice University's first women's intercollegiate basketball team.

[**] Jenna Goudreau, "The Secret to Being a Power Woman: Play Team Sports," Forbes online, October 12, 2011.

TAKEAWAYS

- In leading as a woman, strive to be generous with your time and kind as a listener among your staff. It will take you far.
- Be "graciously assertive" about getting feedback. It's a critical tool in your leadership arsenal.
- Another McDonald best practice is to clearly communicate your career goals to your boss. "Ambition" is not a dirty word.
- Be aware that your subordinates cautiously share bad news for fear they are bringing you problems, rather than solutions. Welcome the bad news, and get your team working on turning it into "problem solved."

LESSON #6

BE A RISK TAKER

"Life is either a daring adventure or nothing at all."
—Helen Keller

W omen who reach top leadership positions are risk takers. After all, taking chances helped them stand out and branded them as forward thinking and visionary.

When you dig deeper into the topic, however, you begin to see that women are their own worst enemy in managing career risk.

Nancy F. Clark, CEO of WomensMedia, Women@Forbes, reported on the finding that resulted when Hewlett-Packard delved into why there weren't more women in the top tier of management in the company. "Women working at HP applied for a promotion only when they believed they met 100 percent of the qualifications listed for the job. Men were happy to apply when they thought they could meet 60 percent of the job requirements." Clark laid down the gauntlet in her blog post urging women to take action, and to do so more often. "We don't have to be perfect."*

Amen! Scads of Ms. Clark's upbeat and ready-to-use-in-the-workplace articles are also available on her PositivityDaily website. She's my kind of woman and ally!

---

* Nancy F. Clark, "Act Now to Shrink the Confidence Gap," WomensMedia, *Forbes* online, April 28, 2014.

RISK TAKER: BECKY BLALOCK

Sometimes to get ahead you must first go backward. That's the lesson Becky Blalock shared in our interview.

Blalock, former CIO of Southern Companies, had worked for twelve years in the finance area of her company and was on its "high-potential" leadership track. But her inner voice told her this was not her best fit for the long term.

She had long held a fascination with business development. But Blalock faced two big hurdles: First, the company had never put a woman in business develop-ment. Second, it was widely held that women didn't belong there because it would require wining and dining a lot of men.

> "The thing women have yet to learn is **nobody gives you power. You** just **take it.**"
>
> —Roseanne Barr

Blalock met directly with the department's leader, who told her that because she had no experi-ence in this area, if she was placed in this role she would likely be demoted two levels down from her current position.

With trepidation, Blalock applied for an open spot and got it. It was, in her words, "really, really scary." Suddenly she was a real novice in this new role rather than the fast-track expert she had been in Finance.

But that was the whole point! The new post required a "begin-ner's mind"—learning new terminology, building new networks in the division, and for the first time, building networks *outside* the company. In typical Blalock style, she studied hard to learn the business and sought out many people for input.

Still, in those first couple of months, Blalock says she ques-tioned whether she had made the right choice. Over time she became more comfortable. (It helped that a senior leader assured

Women Leaders-in-Training:
Take More Risks

Risk taking is critical to building a big, audacious career. Staying the course may be predictable, and it will most certainly keep your feet on solid ground, but it is unlikely to take you to unimaginable heights.

Many Millennial women leaders are almost hardwired to do work that matters, and nothing less. They seem fearless about changing from one role to another until they find the one they most identify with. In my day, they would have been called "job hoppers" and considered to be unstable. They represent new challenges in holding their attention and keeping them around at all. But, they are soaring, and I would contend it's because they won't settle for less than the best fit for who they are, the right organizations for their skills and talents and their personal ethos.

I interviewed Avery Blank, a stellar attorney and a fierce advocate of women. She is a good example of this out-of-the-box Millennial thinking. Rather than climbing the traditional partnership track (which is admirable), she is taking the road less traveled—replete with risks—and building her resume line by line. (Becoming a *Forbes* contributor came early for her because she dared to believe that she could.)

So, the next time you find yourself teetering on the proverbial ledge, take my advice and take the risk. Don't hold on—JUMP! If you land safely, great! But if you miss, even better! The misses are full of the critical truth that soul-stirring careers often zig and zag. Every step (and every misstep) is a terrific teacher worth the risk.

her this was a vital step to broaden her leadership skills.) Her excitement for the new role set in, and she began to see that she could make a real difference for the company in this role.

Bold moves can get you noticed. This one put Blalock on the CEO's radar screen, and she sees now, in hindsight, that the decision was one of the best of her career. As fate would have it, several years later she was sent back to run business development, the very division she was initially dissuaded from joining.

SOME TRUTHS ABOUT RISK TAKING

Here's a close-up on risk based on my experiences in the marketplace.

Being Risk Averse Carries, Well, Risk. Risk-averse people often see themselves as deliberate, cautious, responsible, and thoughtful. Yet, others may see them as being reserved, lacking courage and belief in themselves, and less than inspirational—the very traits that can poison your ability to achieve more powerful roles in your career.

Risk Taking Can Be Practiced. The more you practice taking risks, the more you will befriend the emotional discomfort that can accompany it. I have a friend who, for years, has made a practice of doing something every day that takes her out of her comfort zone. These activities range from cold-calling a prospective client with a daring new proposal to skydiving!

Risk Taking Can Be Vetted. When you take a risk, you are giving up some comfort in the short term for a potential long-term gain. It helps to make a list of the pros and cons on a piece of paper. One column for pros, and another for the cons. Typically, one list will jump out as the right course of action.

Pros and Cons in Decision Making

In 1772 Benjamin Franklin described his now well-known deci-sion-making process in a letter to Joseph Priestley, who had asked Franklin's advice about a vexing decision. Essentially, Franklin's process was a matter of listing the pros and cons, reflecting on them over the course of a few days, and arriving at a decision. It's a familiar process, but I found Franklin's original so charming I decided to share the letter in its fullness:

> "My Way is, to divide half a Sheet of Paper by a Line into two Columns, writing over the one Pro, and over the other Con. Then during three or four Days Consideration I put down under the dif-ferent Heads short Hints of the different Motives that at different Times occur to me for or against the Measure. When I have thus got them all together in one View, I endeavour to estimate their respective Weights; and where I find two, one on each side, that seem equal, I strike them both out: If I find a Reason pro equal to some two Reasons con, I strike out the three. If I judge some two Reasons con equal to some three Reasons pro, I strike out the five; and thus proceeding I find at length where the Ballance lies; and if after a Day or two of farther Consideration nothing new that is of Importance occurs on either side, I come to a Determination accordingly.
>
> And tho' the Weight of Reasons cannot be taken with the Precision of Algebraic Quantities, yet when each is thus considered separately and comparatively, and the whole lies before me, I think I can judge better, and am less likely to take a rash Step; and in fact I have found great Advantage from this kind of Equation, in what may be called Moral or Prudential Algebra."

(More about this decision-making process is available at daringtolivefully.com, "How to Make Decisions Like Benjamin Franklin," by Marelisa.)

Mom's Sage Advice

Fox News Anchor Maria Bartiromo says she can still hear her mom, Josephine, passing along this wise counsel: "You have to have alligator skin. You can't believe the good stuff, and you certainly can't believe the bad stuff."

RISK TAKING: WHAT TO EXPECT

In my own career, as well as among the women leaders I interviewed or researched for this book, there were predominantly two reactions to risk taking:

(1) Some women reported an immediate discomfort (I call it "risk-taking dissonance") after "pushing the button" on the risk. You may even experience the flight part of a fight or flight reflex. When that happens, the remedy is to take deep breaths while counting to ten. The panic will pass.

(2) For others, especially those who studied the risk intently before acting on it, they were at peace with the risk-taking decision and, in some cases, even had a sense of excitement about what this decision could lead to.

Bottom line: Thinking about your style toward risk taking can lead to better self-understanding. Plan ahead, and know how you'd handle what could be a risky situation before you're in it.

Undecided? Ask searching questions like these:

Where can this road lead? Look down that road as far as you can. Where could I be when I get to the end?

What do I know about the destination? How will you feel about your destination once you arrive? Will you feel grateful for taking the risk, even if it doesn't work out as well as you might expect? If it's a total disaster, what's the worst that could happen?

Will it help inspire others? Isn't there something deeply gratifying in knowing that your story can help others step up?

TAKEAWAYS

- Be Bold: Becky Blalock took a demotion to learn a new skill set. Taking small risks can help you get comfortable with larger risks.
- Manage your post-risk dissonance: Pay close attention to how you feel and then manage these emotions with self-care.
- A pro and con chart is a great way to lay out the specifics of the risk and get comfortable with your choice.
- Google "Women Leaders and Risk" and you'll find a host of stories about how an initial risk started a series of door openers.

BEWARE OF BULLIES

"Only when it is dark enough, can you see the stars."
—Ralph Waldo Emerson

The Workplace Bullying Institute (WBI) defines the word "bullying" as "repeated mistreatment; abusive conduct that is threatening, humiliating, or intimidating; work sabotage; or verbal abuse." Through its 2014 National Survey, WBI found that male perpetrators seem to prefer targeting women (57 percent) rather than other men (43 percent). Women bullies were less "equitable" when choosing their targets for bullying: They bullied other women in 68 percent of cases.

Early in my career I was bullied in the workplace. The man who bullied me was one of two vice presidents in an early-stage company I joined briefly. Within the first few months of my employment, poor market conditions and investor turmoil rendered this man's original job obsolete. To keep him on, the CEO dismissed the head of operations and moved the soon-to-be-bully into that position, for which he had neither the experience nor the temperament to run. To put it mildly, he lacked the collaboration and team-building skills so necessary to make a micro company grow.

This spelled real trouble for me because my performance depended on his willingness to support my marketing efforts.

Mom's Sage Advice

Rachel Krantz is a founding editor of and senior features editor for *Bustle*. She tells a story about when, near the end of her senior year in high school, her "schoolgirl crush" (a fortyish teacher who mentored her in an afterschool program) invited her to dinner at his home where—in his own words—he "planned to cook me dinner and seduce me." When Rachel approached her mom for some advice, her mother calmly asked Rachel how she felt about "putting [herself] in that situation." Rachel worried more that she would rue "being too afraid to have the experience." To that, her mom wisely replied, "Sometimes the experience IS saying no." Rachel has never forgotten that: Any time she is unsure or feels she's being bullied in a situation, she stops and does a gut check: "Do I really want to do this right now?"

For example, desperately trying to build business, I requested for his front desk team to ask the guest if they would be willing to share their travel arranger's contact number or simply their name. He refused to help. Bottom Line: The programs I created and managed had to have operations support or nothing happened.

It soon became clear, he was a bully and I was his #1 target.

Behind the scenes, he undermined my authority. In corporate meetings when I offered up new ideas, he routinely treated them with arrogance, disrespect, and downright contempt.

In one chance office encounter (when few people were around), he lashed out so harshly that I feared for my physical safety.

The many times I expressed concern to the CEO, he gave me lip service but did little to rein the VP in.

Because I had never been bullied in the workplace, I doubted myself and kept soul-searching for what I was doing wrong to provoke this coworker's cruelty. I was slow to recognize that I was in a no-win situation. I told myself to follow my tried-and-true formula: Keep your head down and soldier on. This man would eventually come around.

After almost a year of being battered, I resigned. The very next day six letters appeared on the CEO's desk—all of them demanding that the bully be dealt with or they, too, would resign. While I appreciated the letters of support, I was done.

Learn from my example. If you suspect you are being bullied, consider these actions:

> **Document.** Create a paper trail. Keep a detailed log of all interactions with the bully. I did not do this; I merely discussed key incidents with the CEO.
>
> **Consult Human Resources.** In our start-up, we did not have an HR department. We had one very young woman, straight out of college, who handled "paperwork" and reported directly to my bully. I never consulted her for obvious reasons.
>
> **Seek out allies.** I had strong relationships with several of the partners of the venture group that funded us. On the one hand, they could have been a source of wise advice and possible course correction. On the other hand, going above my CEO carried "win-the-battle, lose-the-war" risks. For that reason, I stayed away.
>
> **Make one of three choices.** These "smart tips and tactics" come from my friend Becky Blalock, CIO of Southern Companies. (You'll remember her from Lesson #6—Be a Risk Taker.)
>
> You always have three choices when dealing with a bully:
>
> (a) You can accept the situation for what it is.
>
> (b) You can try to change it.
>
> (c) You can leave.
>
> The last choice shocks some people who expect me to say you can always change the situation. Well, sometimes

you can't. If you find yourself in this situation, look at other places of employment. Dust off your resume and begin to see what else is available. There are always places for talented people to work where bullies are not tolerated. (Read the whole January 26, 2016, article "Bully Busters: Five Tips for Dealing with Corporate Bullies" at www.beckyblalock.com.)

Take a Stand Against Bullying

Here's a down-and-dirty list of some websites to consult to better educate yourself on this harmful and counterproductive behavior. You'll find practical tips to use—as well as statistics to cite in bolstering your stand—should you encounter a bully in your workplace.

- Harassment at work: 52% of women report bullying (April 2, 2014) *www.cnbc.com/2014/04/02/harassment-at-work-50-of-women-report-bullying.html*
- Workplace Bullying: Gender and the U.S. Bullying Experience (April 21, 2014) *www.workplacebullying.org/2014-gender/*
- Why Women Are the Worst Kind of Bullies (April 30, 2012) *www.forbes.com/sites/worldviews/2012/.../why-women-are-the-worst-kind-of-bullies/*
- Bullying Statistics, The Ultimate Guide! |NoBullying| (October 23, 2016) *https://nobullying.com/bullying-statistics/*
- Adult Bullying—Bullying Statistics *www.bullyingstatistics.org/content/adult-bullying.html*
- Do You Have Workplace Bullies at Your Job—Bullying Statistics (April 2, 2014) *www.bullyingstatistics.org/content/workplace-bullying.html*

I chose to leave, and in retrospect, the only thing I would have changed was to have left sooner. And, as bad as it was, that bullying experience taught me some invaluable business lessons:

> **Don't play "small."** If you find yourself in circumstances that drain you of your energy and compromise your ability to do the job you were hired to do, resign. The tone of any company is set at the top. Read the tea leaves and escape.

> **Find your people.** Seek out places where your work is appreciated, prized, and rewarded. Find the "A" players and join them.

> **Start again.** Audit yourself. Rediscover what excites you. What are you passionate about? What value do you want to bring to the world? In my case, after a year off, I accepted a part-time position as marketing lecturer at The University of Texas School of Business. I simultaneously launched a boutique customer loyalty firm with emphases on book writing, seminars, and keynote speaking. My mojo soon returned and, over the years, I traveled the world preaching the gospel of customer loyalty and ultimately joined a NYSE corporate board.

TAKEAWAYS

- Bullying is serious business, especially for high achievers. It can rob you of your self-confidence and the ability to perform your best work.
- Know the early indicators that the bullying is taking its toll. Be on your guard if you spot any of these warning signs provided by the WBI:
  - You feel like throwing up the night before the start of your workweek.

- o Your frustrated family demands that you stop obsessing about work at home.
- o Your doctor asks what could be causing your skyrocketing blood pressure and recent health problems, and tells you to change jobs.
- o All your paid time off is used for "mental health breaks" from the misery.
- o Days off are spent exhausted and lifeless, your desire to do anything is gone.
- o Your favorite activities and fun with family are no longer appealing or enjoyable.
- o You begin to believe that you provoked the workplace cruelty.
- Bad people work in the world of business. Be cautious. Never let them steal your dignity, confidence, energy, or self-esteem.

FIND YOUR PEOPLE

One of the challenges in networking is everybody thinks it's making cold calls to strangers. Actually, it's the people who already have strong trust relationships with you, who know you're dedicated, smart, a team player, who can help you.
—Reid Hoffman, founder, LinkedIN

In the 1940s noted psychologist Abraham Maslow identified the need to belong as one of the five most fundamental needs that motivate people. We want to be part of a group and to feel loved and accepted by others.

"Finding their people" helped make the following women outstanding leaders. Read on!

ENGINEER: DR. PAMELA MCCAULEY

"Find your people. It matters." This is one of the leadership tenets Dr. McCauley noted in our interview. (You'll recall that I introduced her in Lesson #2—Aim High.)

The list of "her people" is long and varied. A teen mother at fifteen, she confided to her school counselor that her dream had been to study science. "Pam, you still can!" the counselor assured her.

Many other supporters, including Dr. Nancy Knox, McCauley's Uncle Jesse and Uncle Beuford, and Dr. Bob Foot encouraged her with the same message, "Yes, you can!"

Dr. McCauley attributes her discipline and determination to her Army drill sergeant dad and her encouraging mom. McCauley's dad was denied entry to the University of Oklahoma because he was African-American, a fact that made both her parents even more determined that their daughter would receive a stellar education. "My dad and generous mother welcomed my daughter and me into their home and helped me juggle motherhood and school. My large constellation of family and friends were central to helping me raise my beautiful daughter and get my education."

With passion and perseverance, Dr. McCauley became the first African-American woman to receive a PhD in Engineering in the state of Oklahoma. From there she went on to become a Martin Luther King Jr. Visiting Associate Professor of Aeronautics and Astronautics at the Massachusetts Institute of Technology (MIT). Today, Dr. McCauley is a tenured professor in the Department of Industrial Engineering and Management Systems at the University of Central Florida, where she leads the Human Factors in Disaster Management research team. Her book, *Winners Don't Quit... Today They Call Me Doctor,* is a great read. I highly recommend it!

Dr. McCauley's advice for women who want to lead is straightforward:

- Find your people. They will hold you up and support you on your climb.
- Find your true calling and pursue it ambitiously.
- Don't be discouraged by difficulties. Overcoming adversity makes you stronger and more determined,

and it prepares you for the inevitable tough times to follow.

- Strive to be the very best at what you do.

CORPORATE EXECUTIVE: MARGE MAGNER

Like Dr. McCauley, Marge Magner learned early on the importance of surrounding yourself with those people who honor and respect your ambitions.

Starting in the 1960s, when women were rarely leading in business, Magner survived her share of hard knocks in the male-dominated banking world. At age twenty-six (armed with a bachelor's in psychology from Brooklyn College and a master's in industrial administration from Purdue University's Krannert School of Management), she applied for a supervisory position that she didn't get. The male interviewer

> "I've met so many who have opened doors for me and remained in my life both personally and professionally. After a while, networking doesn't feel like 'networking.' It's both serendipitous and unpredictable, and something that just naturally becomes part of your work life and your personal life."
>
> —Narcisco Rodriguez, Council of Fashion Designers of America award winner

taunted her, "Can you, as a young woman, make the *tough* decisions?" Magner retorted, "I have the confidence to make the *right* decisions!"

It was a defining moment for Magner. It taught her the importance of building a career encircled by good and fair people who were capable of respecting her work and rewarding her for it.

Self-awareness is key, Magner told me. She discovered that she was a doer, a person who got things done, and that she had little patience for working with people who did not.

She still vividly remembers one learning moment in particular from early in her career and admits, "I did not handle it well." In a meeting with "non-doers," the decision-making process was moving at such a snail's pace that Magner lost patience. "I picked up my stuff, said, 'This is ridiculous! I'll do it!' and stormed out," she recalled in our phone call.

Upon reflection, she knew she must learn to be a better team player—that she could not do it alone—so she focused on being a more patient person. "We as leaders are judged on our ability to move things forward. It makes no difference who is right or wrong. What's important is getting it done!"

With more than thirty years of operating experience and making deals in the consumer financial services sector, Magner has served as chairman and CEO of Citigroup Inc.'s Global Consumer Business. And she's been named to both *Fortune* (2001-2004) and *Forbes* (2004) magazines' lists of "Most Powerful Women in Business."

Similarly, Magner's corporate board service exemplifies her "get it done" philosophy. Her roles in that space include chairman of the board of the Gannett Corporation; lead director of Accenture PLC's board; and board member at Charles Schwab Corporation and Ally Financial. And in the interest of paying it back, and forward, she's served as the chairman of the Brooklyn College Foundation.

Marge Magner's stellar career is one to emulate. In addition to her senior positions at Citigroup, her board directorships include Chairwomen of Gannett Corporation, and board director of Ally Financial Inc and Accenture PLC.

To accelerate your career, Magner advises:
- Look for the sweet spot—a job that you're good at and that delivers impact. Impact gets you recognized.
- Shower your employees with sunshine. Make sure they feel appreciated.
- Become self-aware. Work on those aspects of yourself that could sabotage your effectiveness. (For me, it was patience.)

Mathematician: Katherine Johnson

Katherine Johnson found her people in an unexpected place: NASA.
   The life story of this remarkable African-American woman is fascinating, and I encourage you to read the oral history archived by the National Visionary Leadership Project (www.visionaryproject.org) for many more inspiring details about her. Space limitations, however, allow me only to list some of the achievements of this pioneering physicist, space scientist, and mathematician who made fundamental contributions to the United States' aeronautics and space programs with the early application of digital electronic computers at NASA.

- Johnson first worked in a group at NASA whom she dubbed "computers who wore skirts." Their main job was to read the data from the black boxes of airplanes and carry out other precise mathematical tasks.
- Then one day, Johnson and a colleague were temporarily assigned to help the all-male flight research team. Johnson's knowledge of analytic geometry caught the attention of male bosses and peers who kept her working closely with them. While the racial and gender barriers were always there, Johnson says she ignored them. Johnson was assertive, asking to

be included in editorial meetings (where no women had gone before.) She simply told people she had done the work and that she belonged.

- She later moved to the Spacecraft Controls Branch. She calculated the trajectory for the space flight of Alan Shepard, the first American in space, in 1959 and also calculated the launch window for his 1961 Mercury mission.
- She designed backup navigational charts and tables for astronauts to use in case of an electrical failure.
- In 1962, when NASA used electronic computers for the first time to calculate John Glenn's orbit around Earth, officials called on Johnson to verify the computer-generated numbers.
- Johnson later worked directly with digital computers. Her ability and reputation for accuracy helped to establish confidence in the new technology. She calculated the trajectory for the 1969 Apollo 11 moon mission.
- In 1970, Johnson worked on the Apollo 13 mission to the Moon. Upon the mission being aborted, Johnson worked on backup procedures and charts that helped safely return the crew to Earth four days later.

(Interested readers will also be pleased to learn that Ms. Johnson features prominently in Margot Lee Shetterly's 2016 title, *Hidden Figures: The American Dream and the Untold Story of the Black Women Mathematicians Who Helped Win the Space Race*.)

FIND YOUR PEOPLE SUCCESS TIPS

1. The professional world can often seem lonely and desolate. That's why you need to surround yourself with people you can trust and who will hold you up.

2. My experience is the universe unveils these loyal allies when they are most critical to your mission. Embrace them and make them part of your constellation of support.

3. If you were lucky enough to have "drill sergeant" parents (in my case, it was my mother), rejoice. Though her discipline seemed overbearing at times, it paid off in the end.

4. Be known for getting things done and having a high sense of urgency. Marge Magner understood this early in her career and it paid off in spades. I found my high sense of urgency and the ability to move projects ahead were trump cards for me at RJR.

5. Know your "sweets spots" and leverage them. But don't rely solely on them. At RJR I was a whiz at execution, but I had to work hard to became a good strategist. Management saw the skill gap and helped me focus there.

TAKEAWAYS

- Put your "dream team" together and return to them as much or more than they give you. After all, we're all in this together.
- Deliver impact that your boss notices. It gets you recognized.
- Embrace your accomplishments and use your wins to shore up your self-confidence. Then, look in the mirror and tell yourself, "You go, girl!"

- Be self-aware. Work on those aspects of yourself that could sabotage your effectiveness. Read books and seek out champions—even a wise counselor. Create a team that can help you with these "improvement" areas.
- Ignore bias that you cannot change. Katherine Johnson and her fellow African-American mathematicians worked around it and proved they were worthy contributors.
- Follow your passion. It's your "North Star." Dissatisfied with teaching, Johnson pursued a career in mathematics and ultimately, NASA. Where would our space program be without her and her African-American colleagues?

GET OUT OF LINE

*"[A woman] can learn nothing unless [she]
proceeds from the known to the unknown."*
—Claude Bernard

I was privileged to teach upper-division marketing classes at the business school at the University of Texas, now known as the McCombs School, for two years in the late '80s. The school wanted some faculty with "real world" experience and I fit the bill.

During that time, I discovered a book that deeply resonated with me: author and syndicated newspaper columnist Dale Dauten's *Taking Chances: Lessons in Putting Passion and Creativity into Your Work Life*, published in 1986. The author shares his fable about a young lad, Swift, who goes out into the world and happens upon a huge line of people waiting their turn to enter the "house of the privileged few" (page 22). Swift waits in line for a while but becomes impatient, and he gets out of line. He walks along a fence line that takes him to the back door of the revered house.

"Welcome," a dozen voices say in unison. "Come in, come in," they continue, and offer him a beverage and a chair.

He sat.

"I can stay?" asks Swift.

"Of course. You've arrived."

"But what about those in line?"

"They will wait" (page 23).

I read this fable each semester to my students and it always spurred provocative dialogue about taking the unknown path.

GETTING OUT OF LINE

I love bold women who get out of line, don't you? And when you hear the story of Ursula Burns you'll agree with me that she certainly is one!

In a 1989 company meeting at Xerox, amid numerous attendees, Burns expressed to the executive who headed up the session that she was dissatisfied with his explanation about the company's focus on diversity. She "stood up, in front of everyone, and chided him for displaying a lack of passion and principles. Her comments led to an 'unfriendly' exchange between the two."

The man Burns had scolded was Wayland Hicks, an executive VP at the time. She thought that she was going to be sacked for her outspokenness, but that didn't happen.

A year later, Hicks himself offered Burns the opportunity to be his executive assistant. That chance to see the C-suite up close and personal changed the trajectory of her career. She describes that job as "the most important she's ever held."

Two decades later, in 2009, after steadily gaining more and more responsibility, Burns became CEO of Xerox—a position she held until 2016.

Burns told CNN she was raised to be assertive. "I grew up in a neighborhood [where] you could really be run over. You have to speak up, you have to be a little gritty."[*]

Boldly getting out of line and speaking her mind put Burns on Hicks's radar screen.

The lesson here is simple: Get out of line to get noticed every chance you get.

MY "GET OUT OF LINE" STORY

When I was contemplating writing my first book, the market was already flooded with books on customer service, customer satisfaction, and customer retention, not to mention such adjacent topics as total product quality and zero defects. To get published, I knew I had to propose a book to major publishers unlike any of those crowding the bookshelves. In essence, I had to start a new "category."

I felt scared and vulnerable about making this choice. I asked myself, why had no one else seen this "hole" and published a book on this topic? I was so insecure I didn't show any of my peers my manuscript for feedback. Only when I got thumbs-up reviews from *Publishers Weekly* and *Library Journal* did I start to believe that the book was solid and valuable.

But in the end, getting out of the "customer service" line of books and writing about customer loyalty is how and why *Customer Loyalty: How to Earn It, How to Keep It* found its audience and thrived.

Here are some more examples of women who got out of line.

---

* Cristina Alesci, "Xerox's Ursula Burns: Business is made for men," CNN online, "The American Dream: New York," February 9, 2017.

ATTORNEY NANCY EBE

Take the case of my friend Nancy Ebe. A stunning "Bette Midler" look-alike, she is brains and brawn. She regularly hosts "Women Who Love Business" lunches in a private room at the Austin Four Seasons Hotel and blesses me with a seat at the long rectangular table always brimming with food. The stories told at that table are hugely entertaining and one-of-a-kind. Here's one of my favorite "Nancy" stories, which she shared during the luncheon.

Having just graduated from Smith College (Phi Beta Kappa and Magna Cum Laude), Nancy and her then-boyfriend had a late-night margarita-inspired idea: boldly respond to the grad school wait-list letters they had received. You know, the ones that open with "I am sorry to inform you…" or "We have 800 seats for 20,000 applicants…"

They each decided to write back!

In response to a wait-list letter from the University of Chicago School of Law, Nancy wrote:

Dear Admissions Director,

I am sad to inform you I have many "top-ranked" university opportunities and only one choice, and I will not be able to attend your school.

Yours truly,
Nancy Ebe

The admissions director called her shortly thereafter and told Nancy that she was accepted.

After a few minutes of rapport building and expressing appreciation for the acceptance, Ebe revealed, "I have a scholarship from the Columbia School of Journalism. What can you offer me?"

"Let me investigate," responded the admission director.

Four phone calls later, Ebe clinched the deal she needed: ample scholarship money and loans in exchange for three years of schooling and a diploma from the venerable University of Chicago School of Law.

After law school, Ebe's first job was with the prestigious San Francisco law firm Morrison & Foerster, where she practiced trial and labor law on behalf of corporations.

> "Courage doesn't always roar. Sometimes courage is the quiet voice at the end of the day saying, 'I will try again tomorrow.'"
>
> —Mary Anne Radmacher

Today, Ebe is COO and general counsel for iKey, Ltd., the world's oldest and largest manufacturer of rugged industrial keyboards and accessories.

SALES GURU SANDRA USLEMAN

Another way to step out of line and distinguish yourself is to be willing to do the things your colleagues aren't doing.

My friend Sandra Usleman, SVP chief sales officer of USI Insurance Services, has built her career by doing tasks no one else was willing to do. Early in her career, Usleman spent her evenings calling late into the night from a lonely cubicle, with no one else around, to sign up new insurance customers. "Selling is a law of numbers," she told me when we spoke. "And you have to be willing to do things others are unwilling to do."

Today, Usleman continues her legacy of doing things others aren't doing. It manifests in a relentless travel schedule that takes her away from her family during the week. Thanks to the wired world, a super-nurturing husband and two responsible daughters who support her, it works.

Useleman is always innovating and tweaking USI's sales training models, customer interaction processes, and performance standards. The company prospers because of the implementation. Taking her teams to higher ground comes naturally for Useleman. It's in her DNA.

Moreover, she is peerless when it comes to mentoring other young women and men to pursue their goals. She is an in-demand speaker at conferences and is frequently interviewed on high-profile podcasts. Useleman generously gives of her time to make others better.

LEADERSHIP EXPERT BECKY BLALOCK

Remember Becky Blalock from Lesson #6—Be a Risk Taker? At the start of her career, she took on the budget in the department in which she served when her teammates didn't want to be burdened by the extra work. Being responsible for the budget gave her a better understanding of department dynamics, and frankly, how people can "sandbag" their numbers. That experience of stepping out of line by taking on a non-sexy task like crunching the numbers was extremely helpful when Blalock, rotating assignments, came back to lead that very department and oversee its multimillion-dollar budget.

WOMEN'S HEALTH GURU GAIL PAGE

When few healthcare firms were addressing women's urinary incontinence and loss of bladder control, Gail Page stepped up and funded a start-up to address these issues. Today Consortia Health LLC is thriving with Gail at the helm as Executive Chair. Page personifies "persist, persist, persist."

GET OUT OF LINE SUCCESS TIPS

> "For a lot of women, they think the myth is true: That if they just do a good job and work hard, they'll get recognized. That's not the case."
>
> —Maggie Wilderotter, CEO of Frontier Communications

1. In my research I've discovered a remarkable correlation between the women who took the jobs no one else wanted and the propulsion of their careers. Constantly scan your workplace for those jobs. That's how you get noticed as leader material.

2. Getting out of line is critical to your success. I remember attending a workshop where a woman speaker talked about how it was important to be patient and let others discover your fine qualities. That to do otherwise was gauche. I remember thinking how wrong she was!

3. What I love about the Nancy Ebe story is that what started as a joke of sorts turned out to be her key to betting big and winning. That boldness shined in Sandra Useleman's and Becky Blalock's stories too. Each of these smart leaders used their intuition and smarts as a springboard that launched their careers.

TAKEAWAYS

- The herd mentality is everywhere. It takes real courage to leave the status quo by getting out of line.
- Be bold. Like many of the women you're reading about in this book, Ebe viewed a "no" as "game on."

What started as a fun lark turned into a very big win. Be fearless. You never know what your actions can bring.

- Make friends with gatekeepers. As the old adage teaches, "It only takes a spark to get a fire going." Ebe's letter was the spark. She used her talents of relationship building and persuasion, over a series of phone calls, to win over the admissions director. He became her champion.

- Stepping out of line paired with rapport building can open many doors. Becky Blalock's drive and diplomacy are skills to emulate.

- Useman got out of line and distinguished herself by calling prospective customers in a lonely cubicle in the evenings. Other colleagues weren't willing to do this kind of work, and her sales numbers were the better for it.

- When you see a big, unaddressed need pay attention. That's the lesson from Page. Solving bladder control issues for women has become her business mission. With her arsenal of knowledge from 30 years of doing deals, Page is driving bright, new solutions for an age-old problem.

GO WHILE THE GOING IS GOOD

"If you are brave enough to say goodbye, life
will reward you with a new hello."
—Paulo Coelho

A recurring theme emerged as I researched remarkable women leaders: They left jobs they had either outgrown or were not good fits for from the start.

Fortune's "50 Most Powerful Women" of a few years ago were asked what the worst and the best decisions in their careers had been. For many of them, leaving behind the safety of the known to accept the offer of an unknown had elements of both—though none of them regretted getting out while the getting was good.* Here is a sampling of their answers.

- Susan Ivey, president and CEO, Reynolds American Inc., has thought a great deal about what the most significant barrier is that women face on their road to leadership. When she speaks to an audience of female professionals, her answer couldn't be more clear-cut and straightforward: If they realize that the company or organization they're working for is a

---

* Dan Fastenberg, "Five Questions for Several of Fortune's 50 Most Powerful Women," Time online, November 18, 2010.

place "where they do not feel they can advance, they
should quit." Although one employee can make a
small difference in her workspace, it isn't realistic to
think that an "individual can change an organization's culture singlehandedly."

- Joanne Maguire served as an executive vice president of Space Systems at Lockheed Martin Corporation from July 2006 to April 2013. After having
worked for twenty-eight years at another company,
she decided to leave when "it seemed my leadership options were limited." In striking contrast, she
accepted the chance to lead at aerospace giant Lockheed Martin, whose culture emphasized "ethics and
inclusion," two key values the company's CEO, Bob
Stevens, wholeheartedly embraced.

- Heidi Miller, president, International J.P. Morgan,
confesses that remaining at Chemical Bank for so
many years "was a mistake." Why? Because the
bank's limitations resulted in a corresponding nar-
rowing of what Miller "could get done." She calls
working with J.P. Morgan CEO Jamie Dimon the
"best professional decision" that she ever made.

- Susan Wagner, vice chairman of BlackRock, consid-
ers her best career decision was to "leave a stable and
promising career to found BlackRock" with several
of her partners. The cofounders knew they were taking a risk, but they believed in their complementary
strengths and insights, and they trusted one another
to achieve their mutual goal of evolving their new
firm to assist their clients in solving "their investment
challenges."

Honor Your Commitments

In her book, *Grit: The Power of Passion and Perseverance*, Angela Duckworth offers memorable advice when it comes to factoring in what you committed to when you were hired at a place of business you are making ready to leave.

Consider the commitment you made when you accepted the job. Did you pledge to stay for a year? Did you promise two weeks' notice before leaving? Try to keep your word. While personal growth is important, it is imperative to act like the professional adult you are.

Work as hard on your last day as on your first. No matter where you go next, you have an opportunity to make the most of where you are now.

Never let someone attribute your success to anything but *your hard work* and *diligence*.

Some colleagues viewed Becky Blalock's rise at Southern Companies as a "token" prize rather than a reward for her dedication and stick-to-itiveness. With her supportive husband she was even raising a daughter, no less! She shared with me that her dad helped her put her naysayers in perspective when he reminded her, "Dogs don't chase parked cars."

TAKEAWAYS

- Go while the going is good; the longer you allow yourself to be encased in an environment that doesn't "feed" your professional sense of self, the more you are in danger of damaging your self-esteem.

- Take a hard look at what keeps you hanging on. Consider seeking out a good counselor to help you identify the root causes of your hesitation to move on. Know this: Self-knowledge is power.
- If women are not advancing where you are, leave and find a company where women are being honored, respected, and promoted.
- Learn from your "misfit" jobs, and apply the lessons to find a true home for your talents.
- Trust your instincts. Your "inner self" knows you well.

LEARN TO SAY NO

"The art of leadership is saying no, not yes.
It is very easy to say yes."
—Tony Blair

Making good choices with your time is key to navigating the path to leadership. One big challenge is learning to say no. Were you groomed by your family, as I was, to be a "people pleaser"? If so, here's some help to rid yourself of that tendency.

There are only so many hours in a day, and staying focused on your priorities is essential. Women leaders report that it's difficult yet critical to say no in order not to get trapped in an exhausting pile of commitments.

MY EARLY YEARS OF SAYING YES

In writing this chapter, I got to reflect on how saying yes too often raised "red flags" health-wise in my early life. In the ninth grade, for instance, I spent a day and a night in the hospital. The root cause? Sheer exhaustion. I was a straight-A student spread way too thin with a host of responsibilities in extracurricular activities and, at times, a part-time job. I was my family's "trophy child," and I felt a huge responsibility to make my parents proud. They never encouraged to me to slow down and say no. Even that hospital stay didn't do it. The event was chalked up to being a one-time medical fluke. As soon as I was discharged, it was back to business as usual.

Fast-forward to graduate school. Amid a demanding course load and study schedule, coupled with a campus job that paid my tuition, I visited the on-campus infirmary for extreme fatigue. The on-duty doctor stopped me in my tracks with some prophetic advice:

> "You, young lady, are an overachiever, and the world loves to get its hooks into people like you. They'll suck you dry if you let them. You'll need to set firm boundaries on self-care. Otherwise, you'll suffer severe consequences."

How did I fare with his advice? Not too well. After completing graduate school, I worked exhaustively for eight years getting promotion after promotion. Self-care was nowhere in sight. Then my body said "no more" and I suffered a debilitating burnout that took me two years to recover from.

Feed Your Female Soul

One of my favorite books is *Women Who Run with the Wolves* by Clarissa Pinkola Estés, PhD. My tattered copy is full of underlines and notes in the margins. Estés observes that the vitality of a woman's soul is maintained by finding her calling and then "doing the work." She counsels us women never to let anyone or anything rob us of the time that is so necessary "to feed your female soul."

HOW I SAY NO AND YES TODAY

Whenever someone requests my time, I endeavor to be humble and kind with my answer.

Here are a few guidelines I practice to make the most of my time while protecting my health:

- My purpose and passion in life is to increase diversity in corporate boardrooms and to help women advance in their careers. When I get professional requests, I filter them through my two purposes.
- It's a true privilege to serve on the Luby's/Fuddruckers board. I invest time preparing and participating in that service.
- I love Austin, Texas, and make time to help my beloved city grow and improve.
- "Refilling my tank" is a priority. I make sure my calendar gives me opportunity to do that. Part of refilling my tank is having quiet time to think and ponder. In authoring four books, I have learned the value of saying no. Writing "flow" comes from concentrated, uninterrupted time to write. I carefully guard my calendar, and the people closest to me understand completely.
- I have started yoga and meditation. Download the app Headspace for a free trial. Alex's soothing voice (his British accent is a bonus) will calm you. Promise.
- I make time for people in my life who "get me" and help me be a better person and whom I can help in

turn. Many have been in my life and career journey from the beginning.

- I make room for new friends when they meet the "get me" criterion.

WHY SAYING "NO" GETS YOU AHEAD

Camille Preston is founder and CEO of AIM Leadership and author of the e-book *The Rewired Resolution: 8 Ways to Work Smarter, Live Better, and Be More Productive*. She offers up friendly and practical tips for perfecting the art of preserving your schedule and your sanity. I've summarized a few of her pearls of wisdom here.[*]

Rethink your commitments. Take a cold-eye inventory of all your commitments. These include those made to for-profit and nonprofit boards, committees, community organizations—the list goes on and on. If these commitments are no longer bringing you joy or nurturing your passion and purpose, gracefully resign.

Put "white space" on your calendar. Leave blocks of time in your week so you can think, ponder, restore your energy, and plan. Nothing is more valuable to your success as a leader.

Set clear boundaries and guard them zealously. Essentially, we train people how to treat us, both in business and at home. If you've trained people in your life to expect more from you than you are now willing to give, expect pushback (sometimes it's vehement) when you redefine your boundaries for your physical, mental, and emotional health's sake. Try to take the protests in stride. Remember, you are

---

[*] Camille Preston, "Why Saying No Gets You Ahead," Fortune online, August 19, 2014.

undoing old training; and teaching new ways takes time. Recruit allies and lean on them when you need support.

Deliver "no" with grace and authority. Don't sabotage your "no" with excessive excuses. Calmly, firmly, politely, and kindly say a simple "no."

Saying "no" is a courageous act. It requires courage of the highest order to tell someone—especially a family member, friend, or coworker—no. But remember this: Without no's, you can never say yes to the purpose and passion you've declared for your life.

"Pick three things you want to have accomplished in this job once you walk away. Only three. More than three will spread you too thin.

Write them down, and refer to them often.

Build your calendar accordingly."

—Alan Franklin (then CEO of Southern Companies upon Becky Blalock's promotion to the company's CIO position)

Three Steps to a Thoughtful No

In his 2007 book, *The Power of a Positive No: Save the Deal, Save the Relationship—and Still Say No*, negotiations expert William Ury recommends these key steps to help you deliver a thoughtful no every time:

1. Begin by expressing a good-faith interest in the asker.
2. Follow by saying no in an explicit and respectful way.
3. Suggest an alternative that provides a way for you both to move on.

By moving through these three steps, Ury explains, you have offered up a way to assist that doesn't commit you, and you've left the other person feeling upbeat.

TAKEAWAYS

- Know your no, and know your yes.
- It takes courage to say no. If you tend to be a "people pleaser" this will be especially hard.
- Endeavor to say no to the request, but not to the person. Always leave that person feeling appreciated.
- If you've generally said yes and you are now saying no, expect pushback. We train people how to treat us, and retraining them can be difficult. Seek out a good counselor for support if the going gets tough.
- Be preemptive with your no. It often helps to say up front you are "heads down" on a project at the moment. That can often dissuade someone from even asking.
- Be prepared to miss out. Remind yourself that when you're saying no to the request, you are simultaneously saying yes to something you value more than the request. Both are opportunities. You're just choosing one over the other.
- Gather your courage. If you're someone who is used to saying yes, it will take courage to say no, especially if the person asking doesn't give up easily. This is the cost of reclaiming your life. Be courageous in owning your time.

BE TRUTHFUL ABOUT
YOUR CREDENTIALS

*"Integrity is telling myself the truth. And honesty
is telling the truth to other people."*
—Spencer Johnson

I'll admit that discovering that someone has falsified any credential, but especially those related to level of education, really offends me.

My distaste for that action goes back to my college years. As I've mentioned in earlier lessons, I knew as a sophomore in college that I wanted my MBA and there would be no family money available to obtain it. So I logged many extra hours in the library and forewent parties in order to maintain the high GPA necessary for both acceptance to and financial aid for grad school.

In the MBA program, I found accounting (we covered two textbooks in one semester!), statistics, and quantitative methods very challenging. And because my financial aid depended on my maintaining a high GPA, I worked long and hard to earn my education stripes.

So, you can see why I am so displeased and angry with anyone who lies about their education credentials. It's not like I go looking for fabricated info on a person's resume, but when I see it, it deeply disappoints me.

Okay, enough preaching!

NOWHERE TO HIDE

When researching my book *Earn Your Seat on a Corporate Board*, I learned that the area that people falsify most often is their academic credentials. For example, people make up a degree or say they graduated when, in fact, they didn't.

In today's information-rich age, I'm curious why people think they can get away with it. It's a foolish move that robs you of credibility and future opportunity. In our high-tech world, someone is always watching.

Because of cyber technology, background checks are quicker and more thorough than ever. I had the privilege to serve as board chair for the Austin Convention & Visitors Bureau for eight years. Our greatly admired CEO was retiring, and I led the national search for his replacement. I worked closely with a recruiter named Mike Gamble, CEO of Search Wide. Mike's firm conducts exhaustive background checks on candidates; for them it's routine to match education credentials with university transcripts. He told me that, hands down, education is where folks fib the most.

DON'T WAIT ANOTHER MINUTE TO FIX A FIB

It looks to me like you'll need to act, and act quickly, if your resume or social media profiles currently reflect misinformation. Correct them *immediately*.

Protect Your Ideas

There's a flip side to borrowing from others' intellectual property or fabricating your own. And that flip side is the need to protect your own creative work product. It's a concept I know well.

Long-story short: I had a contract with a company that helped would-be authors craft books. I was working with the chief writer on early stages of an idea that ultimately became the gist of my book *Customer Loyalty: How to Earn It, How to Keep It*. The writer unexpectedly died and the company tried to claim they owned my work. Luckily, I had copyrighted the pages for $25.

Instinct told me to do it. That one action got me a handsome refund on my contract and saved me from a lot of heartbreak.

If you've fabricated information in the past and have corrected it, that's a good first step. But you still have work to do.

1. If someone called you out on your fraud, take responsibility for the fabrication and thank them. Never claim it was "unintentional." All that does is weaken others' views of you and your value system.

2. Be honest with yourself. This is your opportunity to do some hard self-examination. Seek out a wise counselor or friend and start to understand the "why" behind your action. Face up to your wrongdoing and dig deep to understand it. Perhaps you bear a scar from childhood that made you feel "less than" or "not good enough." Or maybe you feel intimidated by your colleagues' education track records. This may be

the hardest, most brutal self-examination you've ever done. It takes courage. But it's worth it.

3. With this new self-knowledge, take a hard look at your values over the years:
   - What values were you taught as a child?
   - What values did you practice as a teen and young adult?
   - What values did you embrace as a professional on the rise?
   - What value drove you to misrepresent your resume?
   - Where did you run amok?

If you've fibbed about your credentials, I'm guessing you live life on an emotional roller coaster. What do you need to change now to give you more inner peace?

Bottom line: Always be honest about your credentials. No "padding" allowed! If you're uncomfortable with your education level, go back to school! There are great executive programs in every city in our country.

> "Compromising integrity is like breaking an egg. There's no making it whole again."
>
> —Becky Blalock, author of Dare: Straight Talk on Confidence, Courage, and Career for Women in Charge

Above all, be proud of your track record, whatever it is. Truth is, it's gotten you where you are today!

One Spotlight You *Really* Don't Want to Be In

Peter Lagomarsino and James Rowe, partners in the Mintz Group, provide research and investigative services to boards, corporate counsel, and their advisors. In a 2014 *Directors & Boards* article they reported this eye-opening information:

It's not uncommon to find damaging indiscretions on social media even from the most pedigreed executives. Double-check your resume for accuracy. That means name and location of your university, your degree type, major, and dates of attendance and graduation.

Please know this: Any fib will be found out! Please check and recheck your credentials. Your reputation depends on it.

TAKEAWAYS

- In the world of social media, someone is always watching—and your mistakes are ever before you. Do everything you can to avoid embarrassments you can control.
- Fabricating your credentials comes with big penalties. It's a surefire way to lose the respect of people who have worked valiantly for their achievements.
- If you have fibbed, get curious about the "why" behind your action. Seek out an experienced counselor and confront this flaw. Here's a poignant thought from James A. Garfield to propel you to action: "The truth will set you free, but first it will make you miserable."
- Embrace your track record. It's gotten you where you are!

LESSON #13

OUTTHINK ORDINARY

*"Curiosity is the spark behind the spark of every
great idea. The future belongs to the curious."*
—Skillshare.com

Bringing fresh, new ideas to the business table is a sure way to get noticed and to stand out. In fact, creativity and innovativeness is the number-one attribute CEOs want, according to a recent IBM survey of more than 1,500 CEOs across thirty-three industries and sixty countries. That's not so surprising when you stop to think about, though. As IBM Global Business Services Senior VP Frank Kern put it, "This is entirely consistent with the other top finding in our Study—that the biggest challenge facing enterprises from here on will be the accelerating complexity and the velocity of a world that is operating as a massively interconnected system."[*]

Here are seven proven ways businesspeople—myself included—have learned to get their creative juices flowing to be ready and willing to take on that challenge!

---

[*] "IBM 2010 Global CEO Study: Creativity Selected as Most Crucial Factor for Future Success," IBM.com, "News room," May 18, 2010.

1. BE CURIOUS.

Interviewing Maxine Clark, founder of Build-A-Bear Workshop, Inc., taught me what it means to really "observe." Here are two examples she volunteered as we talked:

Maxine and her ten-year-old friend Katie were out shopping for stuffed toys, but they couldn't find what they wanted. Katie commented that it would be easy to make them as a craft of some sort. But what Clark heard was so much bigger: a store that was a "workshop" where kids could stuff and customize their own bears.

From that day forward, she passionately pursued the idea, and the first store opened in 1997 at the Saint Louis Galleria in St. Louis, Missouri.

Today there are more than 400 Build-A-Bear Workshop stores worldwide.

Clark uses the metaphor "one bucket carries to the second bucket and then the third bucket." It's her way of describing how one observation can fertilize an idea and then an even better idea. She had recently experienced a two-minute check-in at a hotel and surmised that almost any other business could benefit from learning how and why the check-in went so fast! Clark calls this $1 + 1 = 10$.

2. GIVE YOURSELF SPACE.

Many executives report that engaging in low-intensity activities— blow-drying their hair, doing the dishes, walking—helps them free associate and generate new ideas. I remember reading that Sara Blakley, creator of Spanx, uses her time while driving as a way to come up with new ideas. She often takes the long way home just to give herself more quiet time. Why do these activities bear fruit? Brain experts suggest that rather than ruminating on a subject, the activities relieve the pressure to find a solution and let your brain work in the background.

3. LET YOUR SUBCONSCIOUS "BAKE."

There was a period in the 1980s when I found myself spending time at a University of Texas library near the Student Union— reading, writing, doodling, brainstorming. This went on for weeks. One sunny fall afternoon after such a session at the library, I came back to my house to unwind. I flopped down on a big gray overstuffed leather chair in my den, my head on the seat and my feet straight up on the back of the chair. (Yes, a crazy pose, but that's just me!)

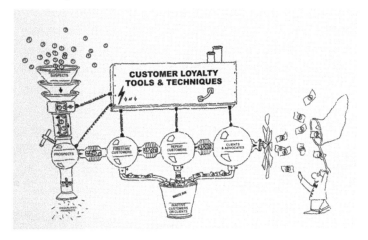

Suddenly, a picture popped into my head that synthesized the principles I had been thinking about all those weeks. I shot up off the chair, grabbed a pad, and sketched what became a series of customer transformation stages: (1) Suspect; (2) Prospect; (3) First-Time Buyer; (4) Repeat Buyer; (5) Client; and (6) Advocate (which I dubbed "The Profit Generator"). It basically encapsulated every principle of customer loyalty that I went on to write and teach about. (That first sketch is reproduced above.) I first tested the model in seminars. My attendees instantly got it! Some would rush to the flip charts and add boxes and arrows to customize even more. Suddenly, new ideas were popping like corn. And soon afterward, the model became the footprint for my first book, *Customer Loyalty: How to Earn It, How to Keep It.*

4. TO CONSTRUCT, FIRST DESTRUCT.

In his 1994 classic, *The Courage to Create*, legendary psychologist and professor Rollo May observes that for new ideas to be born, old ideas must die. A great case in point is the story of Virginia "Ginni" Rometty, chairwoman, president, and CEO of IBM. Rometty was taught by the company to never protect its past; instead, she was to take steps to boldly succeed in the future.

Since 2012 she has done just that, for IBM is now at "the cutting edge of analytics, cloud computing, cybersecurity, mobility and social media. They don't actually make mobile phones or own a social media network, but the work they are doing with Apple, Facebook and several other companies is empowering those companies with the potent analytics capabilities of IBM Watson." A champion of the cloud and analytics since 2009, Rometty is sure to be thrilled—and not a little vindicated—by these new initiatives.

And IBM is also reaching out to new partners. For example, General Motors recently unveiled a new version of OnStar powered by Watson, which provides diagnostics, navigation, and other features while learning from a user's behaviors how to deliver personalized offers. In turn, GM would partner with Exxon Mobil. Watson would alert drivers who need fuel where to find Exxon stations en route.

From Systems Engineer to CEO

Rometty graduated from Northwestern University's School of Engineering and Applied Science in 1979 with high honors, receiving a bachelor's in computer science and electrical engineering. She went to work for General Motors, and in 1981 she joined IBM as a systems engineer in its Detroit office. She joined IBM's Consulting Group in 1991 and began a trajectory of holding numerous and varied leadership positions in Acquisitions, Sales, Marketing, and Strategy that culminated in her being named IBM's next president and CEO in 2012. Rometty's appointment marked the first time in its more-than-a-century history that a woman had been CEO of IBM. Samuel J. Palmisano, who at the time retained his title of chairman, stated, "Ginni got it because she deserved it... It's got zero to do with progressive social policies."**

Mom's Sage Advice

Luci Baines Johnson, philanthropist and daughter of former President Lyndon B. and Lady Bird Johnson, is reminded of and inspired by her mom's wisdom every day. One especially poignant memory is of an event that took place just two weeks before Lady Bird's death. "My ninety-four-year-old mother, who was legally blind, a victim of a stroke, and unable to eat or move independently, had me take her to an art museum. 'A day without learning is a day that is wasted,' she'd say."

5. SEEK OUT THE UNCONVENTIONAL.

Twentieth-century inventor Buckminster Fuller dedicated his life to making the world work for all humanity. Fuller did not limit himself to one field but worked as a "comprehensive anticipatory design scientist" to solve global problems surrounding housing, shelter, transportation, education, energy, ecological destruction,

** http://leadingwomenblog.blogspot.com/2011/12/virginia-rometty-and-case-for.html

and poverty. I was introduced to Fuller's work in a seminar I attended years ago. I remember being particularly struck by the place where Fuller routinely went for inspiration: big city news-stands—where he could scan an array of magazines and select a handful on subjects he wasn't familiar with. Then he'd read those magazines cover to cover. Fuller had learned from experience that reading something unfamiliar opened up new avenues of thought.

I practiced Fuller's selection method recently at an airport kiosk. Rather than choose my usual—the latest issue of *Vogue*—I opted for *Popular Science* and was surprised that an article on the simplicity of science sparked several ideas for how I could make this book shorter and more concise for my readers.

Thirteen Years Old and Rising!

Oregon teenager Anushka Naiknaware has invented a bandage that can tell doctors when it needs to be changed. (In order to heal, large wounds must be kept moist, but checking the bandage too frequently to determine the level of moisture slows down healing and could make things worse.) This innovative young lady designed and tested a bandage embedded with tiny monitors that can sense dryness, which allows medical workers to determine whether the dressing warrants a change. Anushka's invention won her a $15,000 Google scholarship and a free trip to LEGO's world headquarters in Billund, Denmark.

Amy Frazier "Beaverton 8th-grader wows Google science judges," KOIN.com, October 6, 2016.

6. CHALLENGE YOURSELF.

It's been reported that Beatle George Harrison composed the song "While My Guitar Gently Weeps" in response to a challenge he gave himself. Visiting his mother, he decided he would try to write a song from the first book he picked up at her house. He turned to a page where he read the words "gently weeps" and a song idea was born.

7. REFLECT AND QUESTION CONTINUALLY.

Constantly be thinking about how you can bring fresh, new value to the relationships you maintain among your constellation of stakeholders—your boss, your direct reports, your colleagues, your firm's customers, your suppliers and partners, and so forth. As the author of three books on customer loyalty, I know firsthand that the "secret" to loyalty is understanding your customer's definition of value and then delivering it.

OUTTHINK ORDINARY SUCCESS TIPS

1. It's so important that you own your own success! Forget about saying, "I got lucky" or "I was in the right place at the right time." Own it!

2. Great ideas are everywhere! Give yourself space and quiet to let new ideas germinate. And capture them the moment they pop into your head. Today's high-tech devices certainly make that quick and easy to do! Many great ideas and inventions have come to us that way. Take prolific author Margaret Atwood, for instance. She wrote her poem "Frogless" on a SAS Hotel's bedside notepad while she was in Gothenburg, Sweden, in September 2016 for the Nor-

dic Book Fair. "I've written quite a lot under those circumstances. Perhaps it's being in a hotel room or a plane with no ringing phone and no supervision. Also, there's something about jet lag that breaks down the barriers."

3. Buckminster Fuller's technique for reading unconventionally is a surefire way to nurture new ideas. Next time you are near a magazine stand, at least flip through a publication you don't ordinarily read. Pay attention to headlines and pull quotes and ads; you never know what will spark a connection.

TAKEAWAYS

- New ideas are everywhere. When an idea pops into your head, write it down.
- It's never been easier to find creative inspiration. While writing this book, I constantly snapped pictures with my iPhone—a billboard, a storefront, a quote I found in a book. Keep yourself open to the limitless possibilities.
- Creating unexpected new ways to add value to your stakeholders will win the hearts and minds of people who can help you attain your goals.
- Paying attention, bundling ideas, giving yourself space, seeking out the unconventional, challenging yourself, spotting your stakeholder's new value trends; these are just a few of the ways to outthink ordinary.
- It takes courage, hard work, and tenacity to have an idea and see it all the way through to implementation.

How did Sweney do it? She offered me this list of ten key principles that she practiced faithfully during each and every change.

- Show your team unconditional care. Put them and the business first and don't worry about yourself. Genuinely care about their development and careers. There is no room for "foster" children; officially "adopt" them. Show them your commitment and loyalty.

- With each employee, work on one developmental goal. Everyone creates an action plan and then you support it. This may mean executive education, personal coaching, finding a mentor, and so on.

> "[The] paradox of owning what you know and what you don't know is that you actually seem more powerful as you expose more vulnerability. When I give criticism now, I'll talk about how I failed in a similar situation [and] I try to humanize the criticism..."
>
> —Christa Quarles, CEO of Open Table

- Find out what your staff's career goals are and help them get there. Be selfless even if it means moving talent to a peer department for development. Have them work on succession planning. It's the right thing to do.

- When they ask for your opinion, say, "I trust you to make the right decision." Let them talk it out. Do not overmanage. Let them make their own mistakes… it's okay.

- Be completely honest and transparent, with frequent on-the-spot feedback. Don't put it off till next week or next month or—God forbid—yearly! Share with them the good, the bad, and the ugly. They'll appreciate the candor!

- Give your employees exposure across the company with senior management, the board of directors, peers, etc. Seek to have the organization know them as bosses and peers. Be intentional in assuring there are no "blind spots" about them in the organization.

- Have your team define what their "personal brand" is today and what they want it to be going forward. This way, they begin to understand what actions and behaviors they need to cultivate to attain positions of greater responsibility and accountability.

- Stretch them by giving them additional responsibilities. You might let them assume functions and responsibility for or from the next job up. Show them you have confidence that they will achieve amazing things.

- Align stakeholders early on with the merits of an employee. Work to get management consensus on employees and their identified career paths.

- Help your employees imagine how far they can stretch and grow and what is possible. They often limit themselves.

Embrace Your Leadership Style

Sheryl Palmer is CEO of Taylor Morrison, a home-building company.

When asked about leadership lessons she acquired early in her career path, she talked about her assignment as a sales manager at Sun City West in Phoenix, Arizona. Palmer had

> nearly twenty-four sales associates under her wing and most of
> those were, on average, about twenty-five years older than she.
> How was someone so inexperienced, who felt like she "knew
> nothing," going to be a resource for men and women whose
> time in the trenches made them more or less the experts?
>
> Here's how Palmer viewed her situation.
>
> "It doesn't matter what the task is, it still comes down to
> people first. If I owned the responsibility for building a relation-
> ship with them,... [communicating] in a way they liked it was
> amazing." She showed each day how much she respected and
> appreciated their knowledge. Plus, she says, "I had the humil-
> ity to know what I didn't know and not pretend I did."[**]

Despite the bleak picture I painted at the beginning of this chapter, JCP managed to cut costs, alter its course, and slowly but surely earn back the trust of customers who had strayed. A lot of this turnaround happened because of talented leaders like Sweney, who kept hope alive within the troops. Today, JCP is solvent.

TAKEAWAYS

- Often, in dire circumstances, top talent becomes dis-
  illusioned and jumps ship. In these times, the test of
  a leader is her ability to retain her "bench of talent."
- A leader practicing a "Me.Com" style of leadership
  telegraphs to her staff "I'm important but you're
  not." This undermines staff's initiative and hope and
  sets the stage for mass exit.

[**] Adam Bryant, "Sheryl Palmer on Her 'Shoes Off' Leadership Style," NYTimes online, "Corner Office," January 27, 2017.

- Proven leadership initiatives that retain staff and keep them engaged include personal branding guidance, stretch assignments, decision delegation, career goal setting, and action planning.
- What you "inspect" about your troops' performance is far more culture building than what you "expect."
- In good times and in bad, showing up for your employees and championing their career development throughout the organization drives staff loyalty and retention like nothing else.

ALWAYS MEASURE YOUR ACCOMPLISHMENTS

"Sales has the purity of quantitative results."
—Anne Mulcahy

Quantifying your accomplishments is a huge advantage in attaining a C-suite title.

In my interview with Build-A-Bear Workshop founder Maxine Clark (see Lesson #13—Outthink Ordinary), she advised women to take jobs where their accomplishments and results could be quantitatively measured. That way, you can better prove your worth.

That's a common thread with many of the accomplished women I interviewed. Consider these five outstanding examples.

As she told me during our chat, an entry on highly respected financial executive Amanda Nevins's resume reads: "[At GSI Commerce, she] helped the company grow net revenue from $42M to $461M by managing Accounting, SEC reporting, Treasury, and Finance systems to successfully scale the company." Yes, you read that right. Revenue grew by more than tenfold, from $42M to a whopping $461M!

Hala Moddelmog served as president of Atlanta-based Arby's Restaurant Group (an international quick-service restaurant chain with approximately 3,500 units) with annual system-wide sales of approximately $3 billion. She served from November 2010 to 2013. Among her many achievements at Arby's, she described when we spoke, Moddelmog led the brand to twelve consecutive quarters of comparable store sales increases and increased EBITDA (earnings before interest, taxes, depreciation, and amortization) by 80 percent.

Reach Out and Take Your Place at the Table

Sallie Krawcheck is one of the highest-ranked women ever to have worked on Wall Street. Her CV lists such posts as CEO of Smith Barney, CEO of Merrill Lynch Wealth Management, and CFO of Citigroup—and did I mention she's a top-ranked research analyst? She has been profiled by *Fast Company* (they called her one of the "Most Creative People in Business") as well as in the *Wall Street Journal, Fortune, Forbes*, among others. Today, she is cofounder and CEO of Ellevest, an innovative digital investment platform designed to help women reach their long-term financial investment goals. She is also chair of the Ellevate Network, a professional networking community whose mission is to advance the positive impact of women in business.

Having been the lone woman at the highest levels of business leadership, Krawcheck knows what it takes to succeed as a woman in a man's world. In her book, *Own It: The Power of Women at Work* (buy it; you'll love it!), she outlines how to maximize the unique traits that make women stronger leaders, better and more empathetic team players, and more valuable assets to those who have the horse sense to hire them. Rather than "lean in" further or play the game more fiercely or demand a seat at the table—that is, act more like men—women should tout as often as possible the reality that they can take a broader perspective, have a healthier attitude toward risk, are capable of great creativity, are comfortable with a long-term focus, and so on and so forth. Women who capitalize on these traits, attitudes, and behaviors won't need to demand a place at the table. It will be offered to them: not out of political correctness but out of business savviness.

I interviewed a savvy female consultant (who chooses to remain anonymous) from a prominent lobbying firm whose partners in the firm underestimated her and did not consider her "partner material." When she pushed the managing partner to clarify the "numbers goal" she would have to meet to make partner, he answered, "When your book of business is seven figures, then you're in the range." She hit that target and more, and ultimately made equity partner. She continues to be a top biller in the firm.

Wind and Solar energy attorney Cacki Jewart understood that "rainmaking" was crucial to winning equity partner at her firm. She told me during our chat, "Through another woman at the firm, who has since retired, and with the help of a male attorney in Kansas City who had more energy-related experience than I did, I was able to bring in a large client to the firm, and then grew that client over several years."

Resume Advice—Quantify Your Achievements

Nationally certified (meaning her work has passed muster with the big dogs) resume writer Nelly Grinfeld gives a number of pointers (some of which I've summarized below) about how to put your accomplishments in their proper—and optimal—context in her LinkedIn article "Don't Forget to Quantify Your Accomplishments."

- Explain the specific actions you took in order to resolve the challenge.
- Emphasize the beneficial result and outcome of your actions.

She goes on to recommend that you use an action verb to begin each sentence in your resume in which you mention an accomplishment. "Every word, sentence, and bullet point should have a strong reason for being included in your resume…Write clearly and concisely while framing [your] resume around [specific] achievements."

And, in case you do work that is not easily quantified, Grinfeld recommends you provide a context by giving the "back story" of the challenge. For example, maybe you jumped into a department leader role where spending was out of control and your job was to rein it in.

Applying Grinfeld's process I transformed a generic statement such as: "I consulted with clients on investment choices and providing them with a great customer experience" into this detail-rich affirmation: "I established new enterprise clients while also growing the core client base—generating 15% revenue gain and growing sales to $2.1 MIL."

TAKEAWAYS

- While you can't speed up your years of experience, you can work hard and speed up the results you deliver. Make them measurable. That's a sure way to get ahead.

- Observe how other people produce stellar results. Ask for their help and guidance. They'll likely feel honored to help.
- Remember the core message of Lesson #1—Find Your Purpose? It's hard to produce results just for the sake of results. You last longer and work harder when you're following your passion.
- Produce impact. Impact gets you noticed.

LESSON #16

FIND THE RIGHT MENTOR

*"A mentor is someone who allows you to
see the hope inside yourself."*
—Oprah Winfrey

In today's complex and often highly competitive world, a mentor can mean the difference between your success and failure. (It's a thread I've heard time and again from women interviewed for this book.) A mentor is someone who knows the ropes, sees your potential, and isn't threatened by it; a mentor is a guide who has your best interests at heart and will sponsor you.

Be diligent and circumspect about whom you choose for a mentor and you will be rewarded. Consider these three pearls of wisdom.

PEARL NUMBER ONE: FORGET GENDER

Remember Dr. Pamela McCauley from Lesson #8—Find Your People? In our interview, she advised women to ignore the gender of their potential mentor and ask two critical questions to find the right guide.

1. Is this person successful enough to indeed help you advance in your career? Not only can mentors be

sources of sound advice, they can also be champions and connectors. Assuming your ambition is sizeable, does this person have the powerful contacts and relationships to get you there?

2. Is this person truly willing to invest time with you to help you be effective? Can this person sustain the enthusiasm necessary to help you?

Dr. McCauley went on to tell me that in her experience, men were essential mentors since there were so few women in her field.

As for Dr. McCauley, my greatest mentors and champions have, for the most part, been men. Given their high positions in the firms and communities they've served, their seat at the table has helped get me one. In return, I've worked hard to produce results that proved I belong there.

When a Mentor Quits on You

Years ago, I consulted for a "name brand" real estate company in Austin, Texas. The female co-founder shared with me that she got plenty of help when she was an underdog. But, once she and her firm became more successful, some early mentors stopped helping. She tells women who've had a similar experience: "Don't take it personally if that happens to you. Be grateful for the help while it lasted, and seek out new mentors."

PEARL NUMBER TWO: FIND A "DO UNTO OTHERS..." MENTOR

You were introduced to Wind and Solar energy attorney Cacki Jewart in Lesson #15—Always Measure Your Accomplishments. An equity partner at Husch Blackwell's office in Austin, Texas, Jewart was championed by Robert Davis for many years.

When I interviewed now-retired attorney Davis, I was inspired by the authenticity and integrity woven throughout his mentoring tips. Asked about his philosophy on mentoring, he put it simply: "I have a daughter Cacki's age, and I guided Cacki as I would want a mentor to guide my daughter."

> "I had many mentors, and they didn't know it."
>
> —Maggie Wilderotter, CEO Frontier
>
> (Speaking about regularly picking the brains of a range of senior executives in the role of mentee.)

Davis's mother was a math teacher who encouraged her son to work through a problem on his own to get to the answer. Turns out, learning to work through the math problem was good training for practicing law.

Early in his career Davis was mentored by Jay Brown. "I would enter Mr. Brown's office to discuss a client matter," he said. "He never gave me the answer. Instead, he gave me pointers on how to analyze the problem, and then directed me to come back when I had a solution. He didn't just give me the answer, and that stretched me and made me grow." Davis used that template in mentoring Jewart, and she responded by finding answers on her own and becoming successful.

PEARL NUMBER THREE: PUT YOURSELF IN OPPORTUNITY'S WAY

In my conversation with Frances Hesselbein, she described to me her good fortune in having had Peter Drucker as her mentor. Here's her surprising description of meeting him for the first time.

> I was CEO of the Girl Scouts. Seventy CEOs of nonprofits in New York City were invited to dinner by New York University to hear Peter Drucker speak. Of course, with 70 people, I had no illusions of meeting him personally... I was just excited to actually hear my great management hero.
>
> Now, if you grow up in Germantown, Pennsylvania, as I did, 5:30 means 5:30. So I arrived promptly at 5:30. I walked into an empty dining room with no guests... just three bartenders. I sensed someone behind me. I turned around. And this person says, "I am Peter Drucker. Obviously, if you grew up in Vienna, 5:30 is 5:30."
>
> Overwhelmed to meet him personally I forgot my "How-do-you-do?" manners and instead blurted out, "Mr. Drucker, do you realize how important you are to the Girl Scouts?"
>
> He said, "No. Tell me."
>
> "Well, if you go to any one of our 335 Girl Scout counsels or my national headquarters, you'll find a shelf of your books, your videotapes. And if you look in our new management and leadership resources we've just developed, you'll see that your philosophy is flowing through it."
>
> "You are very daring," he said. "I would be afraid to do that. Tell me, does it work?"
>
> "I have been trying to get up enough courage to call you. May I please have an hour of your time? May I come to Claremont, have an hour of your time and lay out before you everything we have developed? All of our leadership management resources, and have you look at them and then

FIND THE RIGHT MENTOR 115

talk to me about how the head of the Girl Scouts of the U.S.A. takes the lead in our country and around the world?"

"Why should both of us travel? I will be in New York next month. I will give you a day of my time."

As long as I was with the Girl Scouts, he gave us two or three days of his time each year!

Championing Women from the Top

Blake Irving, CEO of the domain name and web hosting company GoDaddy, has been a loud and steady bellwether for helping more women enter the field of computer technology—an industry, he says, that's been "pretty unkind to women. Less than 20 percent of software developers today are women. They don't leave high school wanting to be a software developer, they don't leave college wanting to be a software developer, and so we have a pipeline issue."[*]

Irving's stalwart support is deeply personal; he promised his youngest sister, a psychologist and Washington State University professor who died in her thirties, that he'd do everything within his power to promote the advancement of women. GoDaddy analyzes data about diversity in the workplace and pay equality between the sexes as well as how many women are being promoted into senior engineering roles. When the numbers speak, corporate CEOs and presidents would do well to listen.

TAKEAWAYS

- Finding the right mentor is a proven way to accelerate your advancement.
- Two criteria are critical to remember when you're seeking a mentor:

---

[*] Adam Bryant, "At the Top, You Get to Set the Tone," NYTimes online, "The Corner Office," November 11, 2016.

- o   Is this person successful enough to indeed help me advance in my career?
- o   Is this person truly willing to invest time in me to help me be effective? Does this person have the perseverance to remain enthusiastic in helping me?
- Dr. McCauley pragmatically sought out male mentors because there are so few women in the STEM field.
- If you happen upon the right person, don't be shy in asking for help.
- Put yourself in opportunity's way.

LESSON #17

FACE DOWN FEAR

"Fear makes the wolf bigger than he is."
—German proverb

S everal years ago I read what experts had to say about fear for reasons I will explain below. What I learned was that successful people label fear by its name and avoid such labels as anxiety, stress, or nerves. When it is called stress, for example, we often blame situations, circumstances, and other people for our reactions. I have learned that calling fear by its name and owning the feeling ignites action.

Face Your Fear of Failure

Ask any Jill on the street whether she might be afraid or nervous about joining one of the armed forces and she'd probably say yes. U.S. Marine Corps Captain Angie Morgan understands those emotions, both personally and professionally. She admits that one of her biggest fears when she was a young adult was the fear of failure. And no place would that fear reveal itself more than just after induction in the Marine Corps. "When I started training, I was very overwhelmed and... felt like I was behind."

Captain Morgan recognizes that this type of fear manifests itself in various ways. Some people act defensively and others find all sorts of excuses to explain away their lack of performance. "For me," she says, "it was a lack of confidence." For others, though, it's often a case of overconfidence. Still others are complacent, deciding they won't even try something because they're too afraid of failure.

Ultimately, the biggest lesson for Captain Morgan was admitting that she needed to humble herself and ask for help— something she rarely had to do in studies or in sports or other jobs.

Captain Morgan and her coauthor, Captain Courtney Lynch, wrote *Leading from the Front: No-Excuse Leadership Tactics for Women* in 2006 to share their hard-earned insights. And together, the women cofounded Lead Star, a leadership development consulting firm. They advise women to develop an ability to do "self-appraisals" periodically to overcome their fears, whatever they may be. For example, by saying to yourself "This is how I reacted and succeeded in a similar situation," you can boost your confidence. The two Marine Corps officers stress that this is an important skill for any leader to practice. "Remind yourself that you have the ability to influence your success and failure in pretty powerful and profound ways."*

I have literally faced down fear. It took true grit not to run from it. Here's how it happened.

Both my parents grew up during the Great Depression in the same hometown, Marshville, in rural North Carolina. Their little community was hit hard, and like many others, their families struggled to pay the bills and have enough to eat. Henceforth, both my mom and dad lived their post-Depression years with a

---

* Jessica Kleiman, "No-Excuse Leadership Lessons from a Marines Captain," Forbes online, "Work in Progress", July 22, 2014.

grave insecurity about money; namely, not having enough of it. My mother talked to me many times as a young child about her fears surrounding our family finances. I absorbed her fear and throughout my childhood, college years, and much of my adult life, that deep money angst lived inside me.

Then, less than a decade ago, I healed that wound in an unexpected way.

As many of us do, I hit a rough patch in my life, and true to my heritage, I illogically felt I was doomed for the "poor house" (an old southern term for where women went in the early 1900s when they were without means). I was facing many life changes, and my deep money insecurities from childhood crept into my psyche. The insecurity felt like a "black circle of fear" that was always around me. Its persistence was draining me of life. This went on for nearly a year.

> "Spending the time knowing yourself and gaining that relationship is part of where you find your voice and gain the courage to use it."
>
> —Tracee Ellis Ross

Then, unexpectedly, late one afternoon while piddling around in my bedroom, a voice in my head said, "Jill, don't run *away from* the circle; *step into it.*"

I paused for a moment, closed my eyes, and took a step forward and "entered" the imaginary circle. I stood there, weeping in pain, as I allowed the fear to invade me and to let its intensity penetrate my heart. A large part of me wanted to pull back from the pain. But my wise self said, Stay in. Feel it. Endure it.

It took a while for the intense hurt to run its course. In the midst of my pain and tears, I fell down on my knees and eventually moved into what yogis call the "child's pose." Positioned there, I realized I had surrendered to the pain. Not because I let it win, but because I dared to take it on, to let it encase me and run its course.

When the pain had finally lifted, I slowly got back on my feet. I did a gut check and realized I was no longer afraid. That's when I knew with certainty: *I am stronger than my greatest fear.*

How Embracing Change Helps You Face Your Fears

Emotional agility is a process that enables us to navigate life's twists and turns with self-acceptance, clear-sightedness, and an open mind. The process isn't about ignoring difficult emotions and thoughts. It's about holding those emotions and thoughts loosely, facing them courageously and compassionately, and then moving past them to ignite change in your life.

In *Emotional Agility: Get Unstuck, Embrace Change, and Thrive in Work and Life*, Susan David, PhD, outlines these four key concepts:

- **Showing Up:** Instead of ignoring difficult thoughts and emotions (such as fear of failure, fear of succeeding) or overemphasizing the practice of positive thinking, face your thoughts, emotions, and behaviors willingly, with curiosity and kindness.
- **Stepping Out:** Detaching from and observing your thoughts and emotions help you see them for what they are: that is, *just thoughts, just emotions.* Learn to see yourself as the whole chessboard, filled with possibilities, rather than as any one piece on the board, confined to certain preordained moves.
- **Walking Your Why:** Your core values provide the compass that keeps you moving in the right direction. These values are not abstract ideas; they are the true path to willpower, resilience, and effectiveness.

- **Moving On:** Make small and deliberate tweaks to your mind-set, motivation, and habits that are rooted in your values. This can make a powerful difference in your life. So that you don't become either complacent or overwhelmed, find the balance between challenge and competence. You will experience being excited, enthusiastic, and invigorated.

RISK TAKING SUCCESS TIPS

1. To take a risk you must manage your fear. It's really that simple.

2. Fear is a potent force in any career and it must be managed. I like the acronym: False Evidence Appearing Real.

3. Fear reveals itself in unexpected ways. I have a vivid memory of presenting in front of a small, intimate audience while I clutched a pencil in my hand. Early on the pencil broke in two, telegraphing to attendees how nervous I was. (I have never made that mistake again!)

4. What fear are you wrestling with at this very moment? What is stopping you from making a big leap of faith? For me, it's gathering the courage to make a "big ask" to a very important person to write the Foreword for this book.

5. Know this: Fear is a wonderful teacher. The emotion tells you big secrets about your self-esteem and how to manage it.

Bedtime Story

I was a sensitive child and very aware of the ebbs and flows in my home. To feel safe as I fell asleep, I devised this ritual. First, sing two religious songs. Next, sing two patriotic songs. And last, upon fulfilling those requirements, I was free to sing whatever I liked. Needless to say, I was fast asleep before I got to sing my favorite songs.

When I shared this with my counselor, she seemed stunned. She told me that when Japanese children and their parents (mostly U.S. citizens) were interned in camps after the bombing of Pearl Harbor, to keep the children calm, teachers practiced the ritual of singing the songs they learned in their classrooms.

I was just doing what came naturally. Little did I know that this was an accepted way to help children stay calm in stressful situations.

Lesson: Our brains are hardwired for safety. How did you cope as a child?

TAKEAWAYS

- Learning to manage your fear is one of the best investments you can make in your career.
- Fear can stop you from accepting a chance-of-a lifetime opportunity. When your chance to shine presents itself, I hope you'll say yes. But please don't say no right off the bat. At the very least say, "This sounds intriguing. When can I let you know?" and give yourself some time to think things through.

- A useful definition of FEAR is "false evidence appearing real." That was certainly true of my deep fear about having enough money.
- The surest way to avoid the "if-onlys" is to face down your fear. But until you do, a useful strategy is to "Fake it till you make it."
- Invest in healing from your fear by quietly reflecting on questions such as these:
  - What are your biggest fears? (Journaling is a good way to uncover these emotions.)
  - Pinpoint when you first began to experience a particular fear. Did it originate in childhood? How has this fear shaped your life thus far?
  - What life dreams are you not pursuing because of fear? Write them down.
  - What steps can you take now to better understand your fear and help release its control on you? (Consider seeking out a skilled counselor. Helping clients navigate fear is familiar territory for many professionals.)

BE GRACIOUS UNDER FIRE

"Never sacrifice your class to get even with someone who has none. Let them have the gutter and you take the high road."
—Author Unknown

As women, we often must navigate around bias in the workplace that erroneously pegs us as "emotional" and "bossy" and "too assertive." Grace and kindness trump these myths every time.

You've learned from Becky Blalock, former CIO of Southern Companies (parts of her story were told in both Lesson #6—Be a Risk Taker, and Lesson #9—Get Out of Line), how she has navigated choppy professional waters for much of her career. When I interviewed Blalock, I found a warm-hearted, generous executive who has "never forgotten where she came from" and has held out her hand to champion many women to higher ranks.

I was first introduced to Blalock through her insightful book, *Dare: Straight Talk on Confidence, Courage and Career,* in which she shares an example of how to be gracious under fire (excerpted below).

Having just been rehired to lead a department in which she had worked as an underling years before, Blalock would be supervising the very men who had trained her.

It turned out to be a rocky transition.

Before I arrived on the scene, my boss, whom I'll call Fred, sat down with the team I would be leading. Naturally, they were anxious to find out whether their new boss had been hired from within their group.

Fred sat them down and made the following announcement. "We had many great candidates, but because of our affirmative action goals, we're bringing in a woman, Becky Blalock."

In other words, he told the entire group that I was hired not because I was uniquely capable, but rather because I was a woman and they needed to appease affirmative action. [A handful of women who attended the announcement passed the story on to Blalock.]

When I called Fred, he apologized and said he thought that blaming it on affirmative action was the best way to cool the egos of all the men in the room who had been passed over for the job.

Blalock was angry.

But instead of making a fuss up the chain or demanding that Fred gather everyone together again to publicly recant, Blalock kept her emotions in check and handled the situation with elegance and grace.

Starting with the guys, she took every single employee out for a one-on-one lunch, which allowed her to show them who she was and to start to build a relationship. Then it was business as usual: in her words, "measured integrity and transparency, constantly asking for feedback, doing everything I could to make sure our team delivered results and shared in the victories."

Over time, she and her team built a legacy of big wins (and Fred's unfortunate remark was completely forgotten). But Blalock surmises that if she hadn't dug deep to build the relationships and prove her credibility, she and her team might not have been so successful.

Bodies of Knowledge

Years ago I interviewed for a leadership position which I landed. But the interview was a little rocky at the start. My male interviewer, who held an engineering degree, politely "dissed" my field of marketing because, as he explained, there were no tests and certifications required (as there were in his engineering field). "Marketing has no body of knowledge that has to be mastered," he explained.

I carefully listened to all he had to say. Then, when it was my turn to respond, I maintained eye contact and respectfully gave examples of the ever-evolving body of knowledge marketing leaders must master. Then, I reached down into my briefcase and pulled out the three books on customer loyalty I had written and placed them on the table. One by one, I presented each book, with a brief statement of its contents. I stacked one upon the other. Then I slowly slid them toward him and confidently replied with a smile, "Here's my body of knowledge."

I got the position. Someone close to the situation told me he could be seen later carrying one of my books into a meeting.

WAYS TO KEEP YOUR COMPOSURE

Leaders must hold themselves together and rise above the frenzy around them. Here are some suggestions I've gleaned from my career for keeping your wits about you when those around you may be losing theirs.

Temper your expectations of people. Understand that people have frailties. It's a mistake to set your expectations of them sky-high. If you do, you set yourself up for a big letdown when they don't come through as you expected. You can try to enlist and persuade them, but don't expect them to come through every time. People have their own agendas.

Temper your expectations of yourself. As important as it is to understand how others tick, it's just as important to understand how *you* tick. You must be patient with yourself. Don't burden yourself with perfectionist demands. It will make you miserable, and you can never be a winner that way. Remember, "Done is better than perfect."

I've observed that we set ourselves up for failure by overscheduling ourselves. If we are to work efficiently and effectively, we need space on our calendars to relax, reflect, and prepare—and to allow for the unpredictable.

Focus on the present. Be careful not to scatter your attention, your energy, and your power. Work when you're working. Relax when you're relaxing.

Focus on what you're doing this very day, this very hour. Multitasking is hazardous. (See the boxed aside titled "The Myth of Multitasking" that follows.)

Live with an external view. Find a place that brings you extreme peace. Many of my friends, as I do, love the beach and the lapping of waves, and they visit often to feed their soul and give themselves peace.

I actually wrote much of this book in the early mornings, before sunrise, in my "French-styled" bedroom. There, I am surrounded by my favorite things: ceiling-to-floor cream drapes, an antique mirror and chest, family keepsakes, my favorite art, a cushy white chair and ottoman. My bedroom provides peace, serenity, and tranquility, allowing me to do my best writing.

Multitasking It Ain't

Despite popular wisdom, neuroscience research finds that your brain doesn't actually multitask. Instead, when you attempt to do two things at once—say, writing a report while listening to music, or texting on your smartphone during an all-staff meeting—a start/stop/start pattern takes place in the brain. You're not actually doing both things equally well simultaneously; you're simply switching—albeit very quickly—from one activity/task to the other. The result? It costs you more time and you're more prone to make mistakes. And, worse still, "over time it can be energy sapping."* Just like our great-grandparents could have told us, it's more efficient and effective to concentrate on one task at a time.

P.S. Rudy Vidal couldn't agree more. In his contribution to the Huffington Post called "Multitasking Doesn't Work" (posted April 19, 2016), he explains that the human brain "isn't built for multitasking. In fact, it can only do one thing at a time. Adding tasks doesn't expand the brain's capacity; it only increases its cognitive load, or the amount of mental effort it must put out. By multitasking we are reducing the attention we give to each thing."

TAKEAWAYS

- The key to keeping your cool in challenging times is to know yourself well.
- Other ways to manage stress are to temper your expectations of people, to lower your expectations

* Nancy K. Napier, "The Myth of Multitasking," Psychology Today blog, May 12, 2014.

of yourself, to avoid overscheduling, and to practice living in the present.

- Challenging times show you (and those around you) who you really are and what you stand for.
- As women in the workplace, we sometimes navigate (unconsciously or not) around biased employees who want to peg us as "emotional" and "bossy" and "too assertive." Show grace under fire. (This is not simply a male issue. Women undermine other women, too.)
- Always take the high road. Keep your emotions in check and show by your actions that you remain kind and generous.
- Regardless of that inner rant in your head (Arianna Huffington calls it "the obnoxious flatmate"), let your behaviors reflect empathy, respect, and collegiality.

THINK UP

*"It is our choices that show what we truly
are, far more than our abilities."*
J.K. Rowling

Early in my book research a young, self-employed millennial attorney, Avery Blank, caught my eye online. I reached out for an interview and I'm so glad I did. This bright young female leader had lots to say about knowing herself and her values and honoring her personal boundaries. Blank aptly brands herself "Ballerina Bulldog," noting that one can be graceful and self-preserving at the same time.

When I asked how she developed her leadership voice, without hesitation she named these important principles:

- You'll always be tested. Know your morals and ethics.
- Get over trying to show off your smarts. Be humble and kind.
- Beware of [in Blank's case] older male attorneys insisting that you handle legal matters inappropriately. Hold your ground.
- Don't go along to get along. Speak up even if your voice is quivering.

- Maintain your integrity and self-respect.
- Speak up for what you want. You know more than anyone what you want and what your strengths are. No one is a better spokesperson for you than you.
- Start now… don't wait until things are perfect. The risk of not acting is losing the opportunity.
- Develop your network; the more people the better access you have to info and opportunity.
- Study megatrends and develop your career accordingly.

In closing, I asked Blank about those who had the most influence on her life. She referred to her schoolteachers, many of whom had noticed her ballerina bulldog talents early and encouraged her to "think up."

Pick Your Word

Every year Ann Shoket picks a word, and as a former *Seventeen* magazine editor-in-chief (and founder of Badass Babes), she knows a lot of them. They've also newly spilled onto the pages of her entertaining *The Big Life: Embrace the Mess, Work Your Side Hustle, Find a Monumental Relationship, and Become the Badass Babe You Were Meant to Be.* (Not just a good but also a fun read!)

The word Ann chooses toward the end of the year/the beginning of the next, is "the thing I want… to get to, where I want to be." This isn't goal setting, per se. It's more of a reminder about what she hopes to focus on. With her choice of the word "deeper" for 2016, she looked for "projects… I want to dig deeper into, relationships I want to strengthen, people I want to meet and have a real, personal relationship with, not just a business relationship." That word—with all its implied magic and power—has

> already opened up many doors to people and possibilities that were closed before.
>
> As you do some thinking up, try looking up some words in your dictionary to inspire, motivate, please, stretch, reward, and challenge you. Take if from a pro like Shoket: Choosing your mantra-like word "can be fun."*

THINK UP FOR YOUR BOSS

To help you accelerate your journey, I've included lessons throughout this book on stretching for new responsibilities, aiming high, and seizing breakout moments, among other relevant topics. To make these leaps, you must earn the respect and confidence of your current boss. That means you must stand out as a valuable asset in his or her mind by establishing a track record of reliable, thoughtful work.

Many career experts call this capability "managing up" and see it as the means of consciously working with your superior to obtain the best possible results for you, your boss, and the company.

Managing up is good; "thinking up" is just as important, if not more so. To me, thinking up means intentionally bringing as much value as possible to your boss and those duties and responsibilities in which he or she most wants to excel.

Here's how I applied this concept in my first job.

As a new, entry-level marketing assistant at RJR, one of my duties was to track my assigned brand's spending against budget, month to month.

---

* Denise Restauri, "3 Surefire Ways to Make Your Career Explode (And Your Life Crazy Good)," Forbes online, October 7, 2016.

I was assisting my new boss in preparing his upcoming biannual budget presentation to senior management. (In large corporations, any formal presentation to senior management is a big deal, often laden with stress. All brand managers present in a well-planned sequence, so it's an opportunity to shine—or not.) My boss was feeling the heat and I needed to "think up" for him.

He and I were struggling to graph our brand's budget and spending numbers in a simple, orderly way. We tried a lot of different formats, but ultimately scrapped them. By the end of the day, we had yet to find a format we liked, and the deadline was looming.

That evening at home I remembered that in my MBA financial accounting class we had studied the "Sources and Uses of Funds" statement. I pulled out my old textbook, which I'd kept for sentimental reasons, turned to the book's index, and found the term. When I turned to the relevant pages, I knew instantly this format was the answer.

Next morning, I presented my boss with our numbers in a "Sources and Uses" format. He gazed at the single sheet and incredulously asked, with a grin, "How the hell did you come up with this?" "I studied it in my MBA accounting class," I proudly stated. (That class almost sunk me my first semester of grad school. I memorized that textbook!)

PLAY TO YOUR BOSS'S VALUES AND YOUR STRENGTHS

Want to escalate your career? Listen closely to how your boss—and your boss's boss—define value. Adding value early and often is how you turn your boss into a raving fan. The key here is to truly understand this person's definition of value, especially as it applies to you. Here's how that lesson played out for me.

When I was an assistant brand manager in the "new brands" department, we worked on product ideas years in the making. My desk was full of "priorities."

One of my duties was to write the weekly status report. I learned the hard way that this one-pager required crisp, descriptive writing in a disciplined bulleted format. Although my laid-back manager never expressed it directly, I came to realize that he and the other senior managers viewed the style of these reports as a very big deal. I got called on the carpet once when it didn't meet their senior management standards. I didn't have to be told twice! Forever after, I made sure the status report reflected my very best effort.

Know this: Some of your boss's priorities will always be evolving. That's because the marketplace is forever changing. Reading those trends, and helping your boss see them too, can make you indispensable.

Cues and behaviors can help you understand how your boss thinks. Pay close attention in meetings: Listen attentively to what's being spoken and how it's being said. Body language and tone of voice matter in workplace encounters. Study memos and writing styles. Learn to read between the lines to answer the following list of questions realistically, factually, solidly.

- What is your boss ultimately trying to accomplish?
- What does your boss care about?
- What keeps your boss up at night?
- How does your boss make decisions? Heavy on data? Relies on advisors? Instinctively?

- How have your boss's past jobs influenced work done today?
- How does your boss measure personal success?
- How does your boss react to failure?
- Who in the company does your boss respect and why?
- Who in the industry does your boss respect and why?
- What are your boss's natural strengths? Weaknesses?

Play to Your Boss's Values and Your Strengths

Let's say your boss values data in her decision-making process. Here are examples of what you could say to her to play to that value while playing to your own strengths.

- "Boss, I'm seeing a spike in some data points that could turn into a trend."
- "Boss, our brand review is coming up fast. How can I start now to get us prepared?"
- "Boss, I see you're going on vacation soon. What key priorities should I watch over while you're away?"

This framework will help your boss "listen" when you stop to talk with her.

YOUR PRIORITIES

Always be ready. I vividly remember one particular meeting with our advertising agency. I was describing the kind of personal style our customer had. My boss at the time indicated that that "type" did not exist. I carefully excused myself from the meeting and walked to my desk to retrieve an advertisement that featured the young lady I was describing. I returned and passed the picture around. Nods ensued.

Lesson: Always be prepared. And yes, a picture is worth a thousand words.

IT'S NOT BROWNNOSING; IT'S NETWORKING!

I had a distinct distaste for the late-30s' vintage term "brownnosing" when I was in college and definitely didn't try to curry favor with my professors. Boy, did it cost me, though, because I erroneously believed that my test scores spoke for themselves, and that my professors—and later on, my bosses—would seek me out for opportunities to advance. That is So. Not. True! No telling how many internships, part-time jobs, and job leads I missed out on. Don't make that mistake.

Follow up your outstanding performances academically and professionally by connecting with decision makers and developing a rapport with them. Not in an ingratiating or servile manner, but as the competent, smart, and ambitious woman you are. This pays off in spades.

GO TO SCHOOL AGAIN

Become a student of the company and learn as much about it as you can. What is its vision? What is its mission? What are its strategic goals? And how do your boss, your department, and you help the firm get there? These are good conversation points with your boss at the right moments.

Check your assumptions often. Otherwise, you'll be prone to invest valuable "think up" time and energy on an idea that is obsolete from the start.

Have a two-year plan. Get clarity from your boss on what your next step up (or out, in terms of responsibility, job function) is and the results you must produce to get there.

TAKEAWAYS

- Seek out a Millennial friend. That person can teach you a thing or two.
- To climb, you must earn the respect and confidence of your current boss.
- Applying "thinking up" strategies will earn your boss's respect.
- Understanding your boss's evolving definition of value and delivering to it is your ticket to the top.
- Always check your assumptions. They are constantly in flux.
- Frame your discussions with your boss through your understanding of what she values. This is critical to earning your boss's trust and helps to ensure that you are listened to.
- Brownnosing is old vocabulary. Drop the word. Network by adding value to the person you are speaking with.

MIND YOUR MANNERS

"Good manners are the lubricating oil of organizations."
—Peter Drucker

In business environments, manners really matter. How you conduct yourself affects how people view you and treat you. Good manners will help you advance, and bad manners will put you behind.

WHY MANNERS MATTER

The term "manners" covers a host of trespasses. Here are some key categories that I found on the Missy Manners website, www.elegantwoman.org/missy-manners, posted June 2016, to which I've added my own ideas and real-world examples. (Let me also encourage you to read *Modern Manners: Tools to Take You to the Top*. It's brimming with cool tips on how to handle a multitude of situations. The authors are protocol expert Dorothea Johnson and her granddaughter, actress Liv Tyler.)

Here are some behaviors you'll want to be on the lookout for, both to eliminate them should they be in your repertoire and to escape from as soon as is polite!

BRAGGING

You'll recognize a braggart when you hear lines like, "Thank you, Singapore Airlines, for bumping me up to business class!" or "I'm dining in the elite restaurant (thus and so) thanks to (big cheese so and so)." When you're held captive by a braggart, comment politely and try to redirect the conversation.

MONOPOLIZING CONVERSATIONS

According to Emily Post Etiquette, the definition of someone who's a bore is, basically, a person "who talks about himself when you want to talk about yourself." When someone repeats a story, a kind way to let him know is to say, "Oh yes, I remember you telling me."

NAME-DROPPING

Most name-droppers try too hard to impress others; at base, they want coworkers (and bosses) to see them as important and well connected. Remind yourself that you will never take advantage of knowing famous or important people by using their names in conversation.

INTERRUPTING

Only interrupt if there's an emergency. If your conversation or presentation is interrupted, listen politely for a few seconds and then finish your sentence. And try not to finish the sentence of someone else who's slow of speech unless they appear to be really struggling to conclude their thought.

MIND YOUR MANNERS 141

Polite and Effective Ways to Deal with Unwanted Advice

The key in this situation is to reply in a manner that doesn't give away your personal power. Here are a few ways to respond to unhelpful advice.

1. "Wow! What an intriguing thought. I'll give that some consideration."

Even if you don't actually plan to think about it, this is a polite way to respond to unsolicited advice. The danger, of course, is that the person may check back with you in a few days to see if you've really acted on it.

2. "Great idea. That may be just the solution I'm looking for."

This makes it clear that just because the other person prefers to do something one way doesn't mean it's right for you. Whether your mother-in-law weighs in on your parenting strategies or your friend comments on your eating habits, make it clear that there isn't a one-size-fits-all scenario.

3. "That's an interesting perspective. Thanks for the wise words."

This works well when someone is standing over you expecting you to make an immediate change. If you have no plans to change, just come right out and say so.

KEEP THOSE ELBOWS OFF THE TABLE!

Now, for those all-important table manners!

Manners Quiz

1. Do you know the well-mannered way to host a meeting at a restaurant?

2. On which side of your dinner plate is your bread plate?

3. At an event, are you certain what side you should place your name tag on?

4. Do you know the correct way to eat soup? Spoon away from or toward yourself?

5. Do you know how to place your knife and fork on your dinner plate to signal you are finished?

6. Do you know how to place your knife and fork to signal you are still enjoying your meal?

(Answers are at the end of this chapter. Don't peek!)

George Washington on Manners

At around age sixteen, George Washington transcribed a slim volume of 110 rules under the title "Rules of Civility and Decent Behavior in Company and Conversation." (Presumably they were copied out as part of an exercise in penmanship assigned by young Washington's schoolmaster. The first English translation of the French rules appeared in 1640 and are ascribed to Francis Hawkins, the twelve-year-old son of a doctor.)

While these rules are more than 250 years old, they're still relevant in today's business and social arenas. Here are a few of those timeless rules.

1. If anyone comes to speak to you while you are sitting, stand up, though he be your inferior, and when you present seats, let it be everyone according to his degree.

2. Put not another bite into your mouth till the former be swallowed. Let not your morsels be too big for the jowls.

3. Drink not nor talk with your mouth full, neither gaze about you while you are drinking.

(To find more from the first president of the United States's "rules of civility," go to www.history.org/almanack/life/manners/rules2.cfm.)

TAKEAWAYS

- It may come as a surprise, but good manners matter. It's doubtful you will climb high without them.
- Manners cover a wide range of topics and behaviors. Some are just plain common sense. Others speak to one's idiosyncrasies or mental health.
- When it comes to manners, don't guess. Know. Get an etiquette book and refresh what your mom probably taught you.

- In the world of email, a handwritten thank-you note elevates you. For speediness, you may want to first send an email. But always follow with a written note.

Answers to the quiz:

1. Hosting a meeting in a restaurant

   - Avoid taking clients to restaurants you frequent. There's too much chance for distraction.
   - Eat before discussing business. It's hard to transact a deal between bites of food.
   - Allow your client three choices of restaurants. That way you can offer those that are in your budget range.
   - Be respectful of waitstaff. Whatever happens regarding service, be kind.

2. Your bread plate is to the left of your dinner plate.

3. Nametag placement is below your right shoulder. Conventional wisdom says that that placement is easy on another's eye.

4. Spoon away from yourself.

5. When you want to signal you are finished, whether there is food on the plate or not, you put your fork and knife together at 4:20 on the plate as if it were a clock. If you're eating American style, your fork tines face up.

6. To signal the waiter you are still eating (assuming you're eating American style), you put your knife across the top of the plate, with the blade facing in toward you and your fork on the side of your plate at 4:20.

DO YOUR OWN THANG!

"The most courageous act is still to think for yourself. Aloud."
—Coco Chanel

The corporate world isn't for everybody. Nevertheless, starting your own business, building its team, and putting in the arduous hours to make it successful brings great satisfaction for many. I searched out women who are role model entrepreneurs in the sense that they listened to their instincts and have built thriving businesses. To set the stage for the stories I included in this lesson, let's look at a few statistics first.

WOMEN-OWNED BUSINESSES ARE FLOURISHING

According to womenable.com, the number of women-owned firms in the U.S. continues to climb and is now estimated to have surpassed 9.4 million enterprises— 30 percent of all businesses in the country. These women-built, women-led businesses employ more than 7.9 million workers, providing one in seven jobs among privately owned companies, and they generate an estimated $1.5 trillion in revenue annually—up 79 percent since 1997.

Can you be anything *but* excited and full of hope when you read such confirmations that women do, indeed, make great leaders? Now let's hear directly from and about the women I interviewed.

DEBBY COLE

Since girlhood, Austinite Debby Cole says, she was "drawn to nature, and it fed my soul." From spending nights in a tent in her backyard and asking her parents to let her help with yard care, to planting her own garden.

Cole responded to that call by earning bachelor's degrees in biology and history from the University of Texas, teaching a few years, and completing a master's in landscape horticulture at Texas A&M University.

Then, at age thirty-two, she launched Greater Texas Landscapes and has grown (no pun intended) the business into one of the state's oldest and most respected commercial landscaping contractors. Her enterprise provides landscape management and irrigation service and installation for hundreds of high-profile properties across the Lone Star State.

As she explained during our interview, Cole credits her business success and leadership to having a natural empathy for people and understanding their circumstances. This applies to clients as well as her employees. "I don't see people as simply resources. For example, my crews go out in trucks. The truck is a resource, but the three people in that truck are what matter to me." Cole has an innate ability to read people and situations. She can tell when they are up and down, when to offer praise, and when a pep talk is needed. She cares deeply about the Austin community and invests her time—and her employees are allowed to use their time—in causes they all care about.

Cole has a true ability to put herself in the shoes of her employees. "Today's employees face many challenges in their lives. They come from different backgrounds, generations, and their situations change and evolve. They have many options. As a business owner, I have learned to be nimble and to rely heavily on my instincts in making decisions."

Cole offers this practical, learned-on-the-job advice for anyone thinking about starting a business.

> **Find your team of mentors.** "Team Debby" is what Cole calls her mentors. She was intentional in recruiting people who shared her same values and ethics and were willing to support her.
>
> **Never stop learning.** Cole joined two professional organizations and took advantage of their conferences and seminars. She often sought out the instructors for more information and recommendations. Many became colleagues and some became friends. Investing in these relationships had a big learning payoff, and it allowed her to reciprocate and give back.
>
> **Have an active curiosity.** Whether to improve your business, your spiritual life, a sport, or just about anything, Cole advocates staying curious about how life works and the lessons life can teach you.
>
> **Be gender blind.** Cole is often in rooms where she is the only female. It feels natural to her. As she says, "It's not about the gender; it's about the person."

What's next for Cole? At this writing, she is halfway through a seminary program in preparation for an additional career in pastoral care. "I'm taking a great course titled "Spirituality in the Workplace." Author and priest Richard Rohr tells us you spend the first half of your life preparing for your second half," says Cole. "I'm on that path."

MELINDA GARVEY

Melinda Garvey was raised in Indianapolis by wonderful parents. She and her older brother were very close and experienced an "idyllic" childhood.

When I asked during our interview about early signs of her leadership abilities, she chuckled. In elementary school, Garvey's teachers noted on her report card that she "talked too much." Having a similar report card, I agreed with her that leaders are natural communicators.

The first real bump on life's road came when she lost her brother to cancer when he was twenty-six. In her grief, Garvey paid attention to what this deep loss could teach her: Life is fleeting. Make every moment count.

Garvey was just twenty-four then and had moved to D.C. after college to take a job with an advertising agency. She was assigned as a junior account executive to the US Airways account at a time when fare wars among the competing airlines abounded. In part, her job required working all-nighters to send up-to-the-minute fare information off to major cities by 2:00 a.m. to make it into the various newspapers that next day. Garvey excelled, and in just three short years, she rose to group account executive for the US Airways account, entrusted to be the agency's all-important "face." She paid attention: Hard works pays off.

Next, Garvey jumped into the world of daily newspaper publishing (six papers, to be exact) and learned the ins and outs of meeting tight deadlines. With precision and hard work over nine years, she rose to VP of Sales & Marketing of the newspaper chain.

Then came a quick stint back in Indianapolis where she learned "You can't go home again." During a visit to see her best friend in Austin, she was instantly smitten with the city's fast-growth energy and interesting people. She landed a job there as publisher for an apartment guide and moved south. On paper, the job had looked perfect: great salary, lots of challenge. But Garvey paid attention: The fit wasn't right… for either her or the existing management, and it was deeply affecting her self-esteem.

She was miserable, and over cocktails with girlfriends one night she bemoaned her circumstances. A friend, just back from Iowa, mentioned a publication she'd seen there called *Des Moines Woman*. Garvey paid attention. "I knew instantly I needed to launch *Austin Woman*." The next morning she began writing the business plan; two weeks later she resigned; and six short months later, the first edition launched. Now, fourteen years later, the magazine is a well-read Austin institution and respected nationwide.

But Garvey didn't stop there. Her passion for giving women the world over a voice rose to the surface in 2016. Garvey launched *On the Dot,* a global, daily, *audible* newsletter for women with the mission to inspire women and amplify their voice. The e-newsletter features women who have the courage to fulfill their dreams. From celebrities to regular folks, Garvey has a talent for telling a great story well. After all, true power comes from empowering others. *On The Dot* is the only newsletter of its kind: at the click of a button, you can listen to the latest news, stories, and commentary about women in business. It's a pleasure and so easy to listen to during your morning routines.

Here are some of Garvey's insights she's gleaned over the years:

- Pay attention to what's causing you frustration. Garvey started *On the Dot* because she was frustrated trying to put her makeup on while reading blog sites at the same time.
- With the death of her beloved brother, Garvey realized life is fleeting and one must make every second count.
- Life has a way of guiding you. When her friend brought back a copy of *Des Moines Woman* and shared it with her, Garvey literally felt the hair on the back of her neck stand up.

> We may not all have been to a man cave, but most of us have at least heard of such a place. The shed or basement or redecorated garage spot where men indulge in their favorite hobbies and pastimes. Well, now "the latest in gender-specific-sanctuary news" is what is affectionately referred to as the "she shed." Just what it sounds like, your very own she shed is your female equivalent of a man cave. Next time you have a little discretionary income you don't know what to do with, why not do a search in Pinterest to spark your imagination? Next stop, Home Depot, right?

ANGELA ROMERO

Entrepreneur Angela Romero launched her start-up, Central Closeout (which wholesales liquidated beauty and health brands), in 2010 in her tiny one-bedroom apartment. At this writing, it is Number 398 on *Inc.* magazine's list of the 500 fastest-growing small businesses in the country.

In an interview with *Inc.* magazine, she shared that it was especially hard in her industry to be a woman. And being a recent émigré to the United States? "Even worse."

A native of Cali, Colombia, Romero recalled her various encounters in the early days with suppliers who refused to deal with her "because she was a woman" and others who imposed strict two-week repayment requirements while they gave her competitors sixty-day terms.

But Romero persevered. She bootstrapped her company from her own savings, and the rest is history. Today she manages her company's fourteen employees from a 17,000-foot warehouse in Hollywood, Florida. The company's biggest market is Latin America.

Romero plays to her strengths. "I… use feminine traits to my advantage…. I've developed such good relationships with some suppliers that they call me just to say 'hi' or talk about personal problems they might be having. Just being supportive has gotten me special deals that I know they haven't offered to my competitors."*

What gives Romero confidence in the future? "Knowing where I am right now," she says.

TAKEAWAYS

- Trust your instincts and pay attention to the world around you.
- Have a team of mentors, never stop learning, and have a healthy curiosity to succeed.
- Monitor yourself carefully; never take anything personally; stand tall for every woman and man.

---

* Etelka Lehoczky, "From Selling Clothes Out of a Suitcase to Running a $4.2 Million Company," Inc. 5000 online, December 9, 2015.

- Play to your strengths; use your female talents to listen well and bond with suppliers.
- Shake off mistreatment and work to build firm bonds with customers.

REFILL YOUR TANK

"Take a rest. A field that is rested gives a beautiful crop."
—Ovid

I'm naturally high energy and I tend to go at a rapid pace. But over my thirty-year career, life has taught me either I slow myself down or life will present me with circumstances that slow me down. (The latter has not always been "pretty.")

I've come to realize I have a choice: Practice the disciplines required to keep myself fit. Or not. This quotable quote by Benjamin Franklin speaks directly to this issue: "Your net worth to the world is usually determined by what remains after your bad habits are subtracted from your good ones." Notice the use of "net worth," women leaders. His sage words relate to us both as professional businesswomen and as persons with but so many years allotted to us.

Now, more than ever, I understand the routines that bring out the best in me. Although I still have my moments, I am intentional about doing the things that refill my tank, both physically and spiritually. Yoga, meditation, spending time with "my people," reading books that feed my soul, and eating healthy (hey, I still love an occasional cheeseburger and sweet potato fries) keep me happy and productive.

Here's what I've discovered.

Keep a healthy routine. No doubt, we are all creatures of habit. Intentionally building a daily routine for yourself that's instilled with good habits keeps you healthy! Perhaps Aristotle said it best: "We are what we repeatedly do." Excellence, then, is not an act but a habit.

Get your sleep. Have you noticed how society lauds "all-nighters" and working 24/7 with little sleep?

Ever since she collapsed from exhaustion in 2007, Arianna Huffington, founder of the hugely successful Huffington Post (for which I am honored to be a contributor), has been on a mission to educate the public on the importance of sleep. In addition to her bestsellers *Thrive* and *Sleep Revolution*, she launched a new health and wellness start-up in December 2016 called Thrive (to which I will also be contributing).

> "A lot of people forgo sleep in the name of productivity, but in fact our productivity is reduced substantially when we're sleep deprived."
>
> —Arianna Huffington

Here are some of Huffington's sleep tips:

- Turn off all devices 30 minutes prior to bedtime and remove them from the bedroom.
- Take a hot bath.
- Wear pajamas. (Before her collapse, Huffington wore gym clothes.)
- Read physical books, not devices, when under the covers. Read poetry, philosophy, fiction [but avoid page-turners].
- Write down three things you are thankful for. Positive thinking makes for better sleep and lessens anxious dreams or midnight wake-ups.

REFILL YOUR TANK   155

The Danger of Overload?
A Stroke in Your Twenties!

Uber-ambitious Jonas Koffler reset his professional priorities after suffering a stroke at the age of twenty-six. He stopped over-caffeinating, logging 70-hour workweeks, and being the first to arrive and the last to leave the office. He stopped taking catnaps that were his substitute for real sleep. His secret weapon: "I began to own my calendar and live by it. I scheduled everything in it: work… exercise, walks, social gatherings, and even sleep time."[*]

Work out. We all know that exercise is good for us, but how good? Katherine Zeratsky, R.D., L.D., offered an encouraging list[**] that I've playfully interpreted below:

- Exercise controls weight.
- Exercise combats health conditions and diseases.
- Exercise improves mood.
- Exercise boosts energy.
- Exercise promotes better sleep.
- Exercise puts the spark back into your sex life.
- Exercise can be fun.

The Mayo Clinic also offers this note of caution, however: "Remember to check with your doctor before starting a new exercise program, especially if you haven't exercised for a long time."

Meditate. The purpose of meditation is to take the mind into a state of deep peace that occurs when it is calm and silent. I meditate in the morning and find it soothes me and gets my day off to a good start. I have friends who meditate twice a day.

---

[*] Jonas Koffler, "What I Learned from a Stroke at 26: Make Time to Untangle," NYTimes online, September 24, 2016.
[**] Katherine Zeratsky, Nutrition-wise blog of the Mayo Clinic (www.mayoclinic.org), January 22, 2014.

Here are key reasons why mediation is important:***

- Meditation reduces stress.
- It improves concentration.
- It encourages a healthy lifestyle.
- The practice increases self-awareness.
- It increases happiness.
- Meditation increases acceptance.
- It slows aging.
- The practice benefits cardiovascular and immune health.

For a guided mediation, check out the free app "Headspace." It's a ten-day, ten-minute guided meditation. If you're like me, you'll find the gentleman's British accent and style very soothing.

Spend time in nature. I first discovered nature as a kid at summer camp near Asheville, North Carolina. I slept in a cabin where my bed (along with 10 or so other lucky campers) was in a screened-in porch that backed up to a babbling stream. Mountain air turns cool in the evenings, so a wool army blanket kept me warm. I cherish these memories.

A few times during the camp session, we slept in tents and sleeping bags and had dinner camp-side. That's when I discovered s'mores!

Fast-forward to my life today: I have rediscovered that several nights at a campsite in the woods does wonders for refilling my tank. Away from my iPhone (often remote campgrounds have "no service"), the woods and all its sounds, the sunsets and sunrises, campfire storytelling, etc., turn off my busy mind and truly refill my tank.

*** Kristine Crane (for *US News*), "8 Ways Meditation Can Improve Your Life," The Huffington Post, September 19, 2014.

Instead of Leaving a Job,
Why Not Take a Pause?

Do you find yourself feeling overwhelmed, burned out, or stuck? Don't despair. Instead, "discover the power of the pause." That's Rachael O'Meara's message in her forthcoming *Pause: Harnessing the Life-Changing Power of Giving Yourself a Break*. The Google senior account manager incorporates the latest findings from psychology and neuroscience and shows you that the fastest way to happiness is to slow down. She peppers the story of how, in 2011, she stepped away from her job as a client services manager with inspiring stories of the successful pauses she arranged for herself—whether they were taking a five-minute walk outside, spending a day unplugged from digital devices, or scheduling a few weeks off to putter around, travel, just be herself. *Pause* will give you the tools to find what "lights you up" and the ability to lead the most satisfying and fulfilling life you choose.

TAKEAWAYS

- As they say on planes: Put your own oxygen mask on first.
- Taking time for YOU is essential.
- Decide to vote against the noise in your head that's putting your well-being last. For example:
  - A job that doesn't feed your passion, just your pocketbook.
  - Your extended family that is always hounding you for favors.
  - Causes that beckon you when, in fact, your heart says a big "no!"

- o That social event you feel obligated to attend.

- Plan your days around healthy routines, including regular bedtimes and wake-up times.
- Find an exercise buddy to ensure that you regularly exercise.
- Practicing meditation can help you lower your stress level. My experience is the first few times you try, you'll have limited success. But keep at it. It's really helped me!
- Spending time in nature is my newest way to refill my tank. I would never have imagined that I would love camping. But now I do!

ALWAYS BE HUMBLE AND KIND

*"When given the choice between being
right or being kind, choose kind."*
—Dr. Wayne Dyer

Women leaders who earn C-suite positions lace their strong vision, leadership, and accomplishments with kindness, compassion, and humility. Here are some "greatest hits" from women who have embodied this collection of attributes and been recognized and rewarded for it.

FIRE YOURSELF. HIRE YOURSELF

Andrea Jung had been an executive vice president with Neiman Marcus, responsible for all of women's apparel, accessories, and cosmetics before joining Avon Products, where she rose to become chairman and CEO. When Avon was struggling in 2005, Jung says she learned a lot about herself. Friend and Avon consultant Ram Charan helped her become a better leader.

Charan came into Jung's office one Friday night at nine o'clock and said, "They all love you. But in about 90 days, if you don't turn this thing around, they'll have to fire you. So, if you don't go home tonight as if you were fired, and come back on Monday [viewing yourself as] a turnaround queen, you aren't going to make it."*

Jung understood that being promoted from within the company meant she was both part of the problem and the solution. She took Charan's advice to heart. She came back on Monday morning with new strategies and a new leadership outlook. Simply put, it worked.

> "I am a woman. I know discrimination. Tenacity and resilience, with a healthy dose of gratitude and humility, are prerequisites for leaders who are trying to reshape perception and rethink accepted orthodoxy."
>
> —Audette Exel, CEO,
> Adara Advisors

Before, Avon's stocks had sunk below $30. Under Jung's "fresh, new" leadership, the company took a new course. Their stock sprang to a new high of $42.

Jung's Leadership Lesson: Fire yourself on Friday. Hire yourself on Monday. Do some soul-searching in between.

REDECORATE WITH HUMILITY IN MIND

After two months at the helm of public utility holding company Laclede Group, Inc., Suzanne Sitherwood wanted to send a message that the culture was shifting for the better. So she did some redecorating.

That is, she moved into her assistant's smaller office and turned her office into a conference room. Out came the dated, dusty brocade curtains and mahogany furniture. In came a round table where Sitherwood led critical meetings that signaled to the staff a spirit of collaboration and equality. Sitherwood opened her office door and others began opening theirs.

---

* Patricia Sellers, "Fire yourself," Fortune, June 12, 2008.

All of these cues were intended to foster a culture of openness, interactivity, and transparency. They worked.

These small advances drove bigger ones as Sitherwood led two major acquisitions in two years, turning the somewhat sleepy regulated utility into a mid-cap growth company.[**]

Dolly Parton: Humble and Kind

I've come to greatly admire Dolly Parton's musical talents and business smarts. She grew up dirt-poor and followed her heart to build an amazing music legacy. I recall the story of Elvis Presley wanting to record her magnificent song "I Will Always Love You." Presley's manager, Colonel Parker, insisted that Ms. Parton sell the song to them in order for Elvis to record it. The business-savvy singer-songwriter declined, of course.

Ms. Parton is also legendary for her humble and kind gestures. She walks her talk. Here's a quick example.

Female executives in Hollywood at the end of the '90s were still underappreciated. Dolly Parton invited to lunch one such woman, Ms. Berman, who had worked for Ms. Parton's company, Sandollar Productions—which struck pay dirt with the runaway TV hit *Buffy the Vampire Slayer.*

Over their salads, Ms. Parton told her former employee that she had been unhappy to discover that men at the company had given Ms. Berman a less-than-generous share of "Buffy" royalties.

And with that, Ms. Parton gave the startled Ms. Berman a check to partially make amends.

It was a formative Hollywood moment for the younger woman. She remembers the kindness and is always looking for ways to "pay it forward" with other women needing a hand-up.[***]

[**] CEOs Sometimes Use Small Changes as Wedge for Broad Transformation," Joann S. Lublin, WSJ, July 5, 2016.
[***] Brooks Barnes, "Hollywood's Queen of Reinvention Takes on 'Rocky Horror,'" NYTimes online, October 9, 2016.

DO THE JOB YOU'RE HIRED TO DO

David Lee of HumanNature@Work generously contributed this "teaching" story to illustrate the importance of staying on task.

Whitney is an HR manager. She works for a small IT company.

She found herself facing one of the most challenging conversations an employee can have: confronting her boss about his behavior. Adding to the degree of difficulty, her boss was the company president.

Whitney heard that Sal shared confidential information about another employee with a manager. She knew she would not be doing her job if she didn't confront Sal about it.

Whitney decided that she would discuss the issue with Sal in their next meeting, and she included on their meeting agenda an item referencing the conversation in which Sal had been indiscreet.

During the meeting Whitney said to Sal: "I'm aware that you shared with Bill about Arthur's upcoming layoff. I have concerns about what happened and want to understand your decision in doing that."

Sal's face turns red. He says, *"I'm totally embarrassed, but I want to tell you my rationale."*

After he shares his reasoning and they discuss the situation more, he says, *"I understand. I made a mistake and it won't happen again."*

Whitney is well aware that one of Sal's greater strengths as a leader—his unpretentious, nonhierarchical, authentic style of leading—has occasionally become a liability. Every now and then, he forgets appropriate boundaries and says things that shouldn't have been said in a particular context. Because of this, she fully expects it will happen again.

"Actually, Sal... I think it probably will. We've had this conversation before and yet here we are again, discussing this very issue."

Sal responded, *"You should probably document this, shouldn't you?"*

Whitney was both stunned and impressed by Sal's willingness to put himself in a vulnerable position with a subordinate. He wasn't willing to use his power to put himself above the rules or avoid being held accountable.

Whitney told him she thought it would be wise to do so, and to do it with email so they would have documentation.

Later, Whitney followed up with the email and Sal acknowledged it.

This ten-minute conversation illustrates the impact any conversation can have on how an employee feels about their manager. It illustrates far more than this, though.

Here's the effect this conversation had on Whitney.

She had recently been paying attention to other job opportunities, something she had never done before in the over 10 years she had worked at this company. She loved working there, in large part because of the culture of respect created by Sal's leadership.

However, the last couple of years had been tough, with economic and marketplace shifts forcing the company to reduce hours and salaries. The tumult had made her less confident about the company's future and led her to question if she would be wise to explore alternatives.

This conversation changed everything. Whitney decided to stay with the company. She saw that her values aligned with Sal's leadership values and decided to stay.

Lee's Employment Lesson: Having the confidence to call your boss on an infraction is a huge risk. Think about situations you could find yourself in. How would you react?

REALLY LISTEN TO EMPLOYEES

Your employees are a great source of ideas. They are the ones out in the field, on the phones with customers, doing online chats. These "listening posts" are a treasure chest of how to improve processes and serve customers better.

Here's a story about a savvy woman leader who did just that.****

Shari Ballard, a twenty-three-year Best Buy veteran who oversees all the company's domestic stores, listens to her field employees.

In 2014 and 2015 Chris Schmidt was Best Buy's Colorado market director and he and his team were consistently showing increased sales despite having fewer customers at their stores. Schmidt's secret was using a spreadsheet he created into which he plugged employees' scores across all the performance metrics the company tracked. Of course, those measures didn't matter if his staff weren't closing sales, so he sorted the spreadsheet so that those lagging behind would be easily spotted and thereafter targeted for further education. For instance, some might need to be trained more on the newest, most sophisticated models of TVs being offered; others might need practice in how to open conversations with prospective buyers without scaring them off. "Even tiny bits of movement yield massive amounts of return," Schmidt says of those behavioral tweaks, which could increase a single employee's sales by tens of thousands of dollars a year.

Ballard decided to incorporate Schmidt's spreadsheet tool more broadly after witnessing it in action. By Thanksgiving 2016, she had seen to it that every one of Best Buy's 2,000 store leaders had completed a data-driven training program

---
**** Jen Wieczner, "Meet the Women Who Saved Best Buy," Fortune online, October 25, 2015.

they call "Individual Sales Tracker." (She also decided to promote Schmidt to vice president of sales operations.) Sys Ballard: "What's the biggest difference, and why are the stores growing? I would say: *that*,"

MANAGE BY WALKING AROUND

William Hewlett and David Packard, founders of Hewlett Packard (HP), famously used this approach. Nothing lifts employee morale more than being face-to-face with their leader. Walk around, smile, observe, be approachable, and call employees by name. Show them you know them and care about them.

When I visited the unforgettable National 9/11 Memorial and Museum in NYC, I sat in a listening room where families and friends had recorded heartwarming stories of their lost loved ones. A mother told the story of her daughter who had loved her job and sat near her CEO's office. She devised a clever plan to get on his radar screen. She noted that his favorite candy was jellybeans and she stocked them in a big glass jar on her desk. To her delight, the CEO routinely stopped by for a short hello and a treat. He spoke at her funeral and told this story that her mother so fondly remembered.

BE RESPECTFUL OF OTHERS' TIME

Show your bosses, managers, and peers that you value their time by arriving on time for meetings. This applies to conference calls as well.

I was recently on two consecutive conference calls with the same organizational leader, and each time he joined the call ten minutes late, causing the rest of us to have to wait. Each time he had an excuse, but for me, his behavior suggested a lack of consideration for everyone else on the call.

Humility is not shown by words, but by actions.

ALWAYS SAY PLEASE AND THANK YOU

As simple as it sounds, "please" and "thank you" telegraph humility and respect.

As a leader, you set the tone for your team. Besides saying please and thank you, consider jotting notes of appreciation on well-done reports.

I recall a story that Peggy Noonan told about herself. Having just moved from a position as a producer at CBS, she was finding her way in a completely new job as speechwriter for President Ronald Reagan in the formidable White House. She received a "well done!" in the president's handwriting on an early assignment. Noonan tore off the compliment, taped it to her person, and wore it proudly around the office all day.

While we can't all get kudos from America's commander-in-chief, as a leader-in-the-making you can show genuine appreciation to those around you. It matters. It's a powerful tool for earning support and respect. Say please and thank you often!

TAKEAWAYS

- Compassion, kindness, and humility are critical leadership skills.
- When you show your employees you care about them, they stay engaged, perform well, and spread the word about your leadership style.
- Humility and compassion are demonstrated through your actions, not your words.
- Shifting culture, calling out mistakes, showing consideration for others' time, managing by walking around, and really listening to employees are a few ways to exemplify compassionate leadership.

WHO'S YOUR HERO?

"Generally speaking, men are held in great esteem in all parts of the world, so why shouldn't women have their share? Soldiers and war heroes are honored and commemorated, explorers are granted immortal fame, martyrs are revered, but how many people look upon women too as soldiers?"
—Anne Frank

With each lesson I wrote in this book, the message grew louder and stronger that women are great leaders. But I also realized that it's not only women who are. Men who support women leaders, and who are attuned to and nurture traits within themselves that are generally attributed to women (communication skills, emotional intelligence, efficiency, tenacity), serve as role models too.

My hero is the late Air Force General Robert Herres, chairman of USAA, the insurance and asset management corporation for members of the military. I came to know this great man when he agreed to write the foreword for the second edition of my book *Customer Loyalty: How to Earn It, How to Keep It.*

General Herres represented the greatness of America and showed how someone from ordinary circumstances could apply himself and become extraordinary. He served his country, community, and family with character, dignity, and deep devotion.

He is my hero for many reasons. He led through example and with these directives:

- One is never too old to welcome new friends into their life, as he welcomed me.
- Respect "rank" and take business matters up the chain of command.
- Be informed about our Founding Fathers and honor and respect their brilliance for sculpting the freedoms we enjoy today. He wrote about General George Washington's loyalty to his troops, and they to him, and what loyalty means to contemporary business.
- Have a deep faith in God. As his life was ending, he remained upbeat, positive, and in awe of his doctors. He loved bragging to me about the competency of his female oncologist!
- Pay keen attention to details in growing a business. That included welcoming guests. When I arrived at the Pentagon-size headquarters in San Antonio for my first meeting with General Herres, a beautiful drive led me to the parking area, where I was greeted by a beautifully lettered sign in a visitor's space that read: "Welcome Jill Griffin."
- Champion your employees. When a USAA employee worked late, it bothered him that the last thing he or she would see was a security agent "packing up" for the night. He told me USAA employees "deserved better." (And he quickly remedied this situation!)
- When a business is in trouble, find the best talent to turn it around. As chairman of Luby's, he personally

recruited highly respected Houston restaurant entrepreneurs Chris and Harris Pappas, who brought life
back to the beloved Luby's brand.

- Take great pride in family. He shared with me
  numerous happy anecdotes of how he and his wife,
  Shirley, raised their children.
- Build a stellar career, yet be humble about your
  accomplishments. Much of what I know about his
  accomplishments I had to research on my own.

What Mary Tyler Moore Taught Women Leaders

Another one of my heroes is Mary Tyler Moore, who both in her television roles and in her personal life was an important role model for me as I zigged and zagged through my early career.
Here are eight principles she reinforced for me.

1. Smile… it's the shortest distance between two people.

2. Always be humble and kind. She was considerate of all who surrounded her.

3. Do your homework. Nothing succeeds like brains and brawn.

4. Enthusiasm is contagious. People love the vibe of enthusiasm and are attracted to those who have it.

5. Respect your boss and your colleagues…even when they can be a bit nutty!

6. Tragedy can strike anyone. (In her real life, she lost her young son to a self-inflicted gunshot wound that was ruled accidental.)

7. Take risks. On TV and in her professional life, she took risks. Her role in the Robert Redford–directed film *Ordinary People* was a far cry from her usual comedy.
   She received great acclaim for her performance.

8. Humor is a career enhancer. Choose your moments and inject a funny.

Thanks, Mary Tyler Moore! Rest in peace.

If you're fortunate in life, you've been embraced by such a hero. Maybe it was your mom, a sports coach, your scout leader, a special teacher, or an amazing friend—just to name a few.

And as I wrap up, I ask you to ponder who your hero is. It matters. If you know the person, write a note and say thank you.

And, above all, do good deeds and kindnesses in the world. Who knows? You may become a hero in someone else's life.

TAKEAWAYS

- Every day, the challenges and experiences you face can be surprising input for making you a better leader.
- A common thread in this book is that leaders are always questing to be a better version of their at-the-moment self.

GET STARTED

Now it's time to get your ball rolling! You've just read twenty-five lessons learned from but a handful of the women who are great leaders in their respective corners of the world. Pick one that you feel particularly passionate about and get going.

For example, consider Lesson #5—Insist on Feedback. Apply these four steps:

1. Brainstorm: Take out a sheet of paper and map the constellation of people whose feedback is critical to your leadership rise. Group them in "packs"— friends, family, colleagues, bosses, subordinates, and so forth.

2. Prioritize: Pick your most valuable "Top 10." (Those folks whose feedback is essential to your career rise.)

3. Plan: Strategize how to get feedback early and often from your list. In regard to your bosses, endeavor to pay close attention to what they value in your performance and look for ways to provide them with more of your good stuff!

4. Act: Step out. Receive and give your best. This includes thanking each person who gives you feedback for his or her candor and kindness in helping you grow. We're taught to start a project from its beginning. Experience has taught me otherwise. When I

embarked on writing my first book, *Customer Loyalty: How to Earn It, How to Keep It*, I began with Chapter Three. Why? I knew the content well and the writing flowed. Success with that chapter, in turn, gave me confidence to tackle the more difficult chapters.

A LITTLE INSPIRATION AS WE CLOSE…

When I was a little girl, my mom put me in dance lessons. I loved it! We'd wear our leotard and tap shoes (tied with bright-pink luminous laces) and practice our routines in anticipation of the "show" we'd put on for our parents.

The opening song's lyrics went something like this…

"This is time, this is the show, we're full of pep and we're set to go. We're singing for you… we're dancing for you… especially for you—you wonderful people!!!"

As we wrap up, I hope these twenty-four lessons have inspired you to embrace your talents, continually sharpen them, and show the world what you've got!!

I'll be cheering you on!

LOOK FOR US!

I am pleased to be the Austin affiliate for 2020 Women on Boards.

The logic is simple and clear: For us to be globally competitive, we need to use all the talent available to us—both female and male. http://jillgriffin.net/women-boards-2020/

ACKNOWLEDGMENTS

I am always humbled by how many talented hands touch my manuscript as it's being shaped and formed.

Special thanks to my editor, Linda O'Doughda; Draft Lab (Alex Head and Lari Bishop); publicist, Dennis and his right arm, Susie Welch; Cheryl Rae and the "always there" Ray Bard.

And a big "thumbs up" to my adventurous boyfriend, Doug Glasgow, who has most recently introduced me to electric bikes!

I am especially grateful to these women leaders who so generously shared their inspiring stories.

Becky Blalock

Avery Blank

Maxine Clark

Dr. Imogen Coe

Debby Cole

Nancy Ebe

Melinda Garvey

Frances Hesselbein

Sheila Hooda

Cacki Jewart

Marge Magner

Dr. Pamela McCauley

Jamie McDonald

Martha McGill

Hala Moddelmog

Amanda Nevins

Gail Page

Karen Rogge

Liz Sweney

Sandra Usleman

Kim Wyant

WOMEN MAKE GREAT LEADERS RESOURCES (AND OTHER GOOD READS)

So much to read and so little time! That's especially true in our information-inundated times, don't you think? But I'm hoping that the topics I've covered in this book have sparked your interest and desire to delve into them further. And to help you with that, I've jotted down this quick and easy (but by no means comprehensive) list of authors and their current books (check out their earlier works, too, of course, if they've written several) whose messages are well worth listening to. (Spoiler alert: I guarantee that you won't always agree with what you read. But part of being a great leader is tackling an issue from many different perspectives and showing respect to others, right?)

COPYRIGHT 2017

Sallie Krawcheck, *Own It: The Power of Women at Work*

Angie Morgan and Courtney Lynch, *Leading from the Front: No-Excuse Leadership Tactics for Women*

Amy Morin, *13 Things Mentally Strong People Don't Do: Take Back Your Power, Embrace Change, Face Your Fears, and Train Your Brain for Happiness and Success*

Pat Obuchowski, *Gutsy Women Win: Hot to Get Gutsy and Get Going*

Rachael O'Meara, *Pause: Harnessing the Life-Changing Power of Giving Yourself a Break*

Ann Shoket, *The Big Life: Embrace the Mess, Work Your Side Hustle, Find a Monumental Relationship, and Become the Badass Babe You Were Meant to Be*

Jen Sincero, *You Are a Badass at Making Money: Master the Mindset of Wealth*

Julia Storberg-Walker and Paige Haber-Curran, *Theorizing Women and Leadership: New Insights and Contributions from Multiple Perspectives*

COPYRIGHT 2016

Sylvia Becker-Hill, *12 Leadership Powers for Successful Women*

Jessica Bennett, *Feminist Fight Club: An Office Survival Manual (for a Sexist Workplace)*

Jenny Blake, *Pivot: The Only Move That Matters Is Your Next One*

Susan David, PhD, *Emotional Agility: Get Unstuck, Embrace Change, and Thrive in Work and Life*

Therese Huston, *How Women Decide: What's True, What's Not, and What Strategies Spark the Best Choices*

Grace Killelea, *The Confidence Effect: Every Woman's Guide to the Attitude That Attracts Success*

Jonathan Kis-Lev, *Brag Woman, Brag! What Women Still Need to Learn in Order to Get the Opportunities You Deserve*

Margot Lee Shetterly, *Hidden Figures: The American Dream and the Untold Story of the Black Women Mathematicians Who Helped Win the Space Race*

Nina Tassler (editor), *What I Told My Daughter: Lessons from Leaders on Raising the Next Generation of Empowered Women*

Andrea Tantaros, *Tied Up in Knots: How Getting What We Wanted Made Women Miserable*

Rosamund Stone Zander, *Pathways to Possibility: Transforming Our Relationship with Ourselves, Each Other, and the World*

COPYRIGHT 2015

Chimamanda Ngozi Adichie, *We Should All Be Feminists*

Peter F. Drucker and Frances Hesselbein, *Peter Drucker's Five Most Important Questions: Enduring Wisdom for Today's Leaders*

Kirsten Gillibrand (foreword by Hillary R. Clinton), *Off the Sidelines: Speak Up, Be Fearless, and Change Your World*

Arianna Huffington, *Thrive: The Third Metric to Redefining Success and Creating a Life of Well-Being, Wisdom, and Wonder*

Jack and Suzy Welch, *The Real-Life MBA: Your No-BS Guide to Winning the Game, Building a Team, and Growing Your Career*

COPYRIGHT 2014

Lois Frankel, PhD, *Nice Girls Still Don't Get the Corner Office: Unconscious Mistakes Women Make That Sabotage Their Careers*

Katty Kay & Claire Shipman, *The Confidence Code: The Science and Art of Self-Assurance—What Women Should Know*

Nancy D. O'Reilly, PsyD, *Leading Women: 20 Influential Women Share Their Secrets to Leadership, Business, and Life*

COPYRIGHT 2013

Dorie Clark, *Reinventing You: Define Your Brand, Imagine Your Future*

Frances Hesselbein and Jim Collins, *Hesselbein on Leadership*

Dorothea Johnson and Liv Tyler, *Modern Manners: Tools to Take You to the Top*

Marianne Schnall, *What Will It Take to Make a Woman President? Conversations About Women, Leadership, and Power*

Jen Sincero, *You Are a Badass: How to Stop Doubting Your Greatness and Start Living an Awesome Life*

Teresa A. Taylor, *The Balance Myth: Rethinking Work-Life Success*

COPYRIGHT 2012

Olivia Fox Cabane, *The Charisma Myth: How Anyone Can Master the Art and Science of Personal Magnetism*

Camille Preston, *The Rewired Resolution: 8 Ways to Work Smarter, Live Better, and Be More Productive.*

COPYRIGHT 2011

Heidi Grant Halvorson, PhD, *Succeed: How We Can Reach Our Goals*

Frances Hesselbein, *My Life in Leadership: The Journey and Lessons Learned Along the Way*

Susan T. Spencer, *Briefcase Essentials: Discover Your 12 Natural Talents for Achieving Success in a Male-Dominated Workplace*

COPYRIGHT 2010

Chin-Ning chu, *The Art of War for Women: Sun Tzu's Ultimate Guide to Winning without Confrontation*

Gail Collins, *When Everything Changed: The Amazing Journey of American Women from 1960 to the Present*

INDEX

ABOUT THE AUTHOR

Jill is NACD corporate governance fellow and independent board director for Luby's/Fuddruckers (NYSE: LUB.) She is leading Austin Texas WomenBoards 2020, a national initiative to ensure women hold 20% of the seats on corporate boards by 2020.

Since 1988 she has steered JJ Griffin Inc. through challenging and fun assignments including chairing VisitAustin.org for eight years.

Jill's first book *Customer Loyalty* was selected as a Harvard "Working Knowledge" title and became an international best seller.

Jill is a magna cum laude graduate, fellowship recipient and Distinguished Alumna of the University of South Carolina Moore School of Business where she earned her undergraduate and MBA degrees.

Jill began her career in brand management at R.J Reynolds Tobacco Company where she rose to manage the corporation's largest brand, Winston.

Jill's hobbies include camping, biking, yoga and American history, and acrylic painting. Check out her art gallery at http://jillgriffin.net/about/artwork/.

This is Jill's fifth book.